THE MAN
WHO SOLD A GHOST

Chinese Tales of the 3rd-6th Centuries

Fredonia Books
Amsterdam, The Netherlands

The Man Who Sold a Ghost:
Chinese Tales of the 3rd-6th Centuries

Translated by
Hsien-Yi Yang
Gladys Yang

ISBN: 1-4101-0222-X

Reprinted from the 1958 edition

Fredonia Books
Amsterdam, The Netherlands
http://www.fredoniabooks.com

FOREWORD

This collection contains some of the best Chinese tales from the third to the sixth century.

They fall into two main categories: stories of the supernatural and anecdotes about historical figures. The former, which clearly predominate, evolved from earlier myths and legends.

Lu Hsun said in his *Brief History of Chinese Fiction*: "When primitive men were puzzled by the ever-changing phenomena of nature, they made stories to explain them. And so myths started." As society developed, myths changed into legends. The chief characters in myths are gods, while in legends they are men with semi-divine qualities. The ancient myths and legends of China have not been preserved because the ruling class neglected them; but occasional examples can be found in old works of philosophy or history. Thus the *Book of Mountains and Seas* has preserved many myths and legends of bygone heroes. Another work of the Warring States Period, the *Travels of King Mu*, records how this Chou dynasty king journeyed in a carriage drawn by eight divine horses to the Queen Mother of the West. The ghost and fairy stories of the third to the sixth century were inspired by the spirit we find in those early myths and legends.

Since the old myths and legends were closely linked with ancient history, the earliest historical records often include them as authentic facts. Later legends parted company with myths and became more like modern stories. This collection also includes anecdotes about real men — another type of early Chinese fiction.

Though the tales about the supernatural originated in myths and legends, they possess a distinctive social content and a fair degree of realism.

At the end of the Han dynasty the famous Yellow Turban Revolt broke out as a result of the cruel exploitation of the people. After the failure of this revolt the empire was split into three kingdoms. During the fighting among different warlords, hundreds of thousands of people were killed, pestilence and famine were rife, and farms were laid waste. This was a dark age for China. After the establishment of the Western Tsin dynasty, the empire had not been united long when there was trouble with the various princes. Then followed invasions by nomadic tribes from the north. The house of Tsin moved south of the Yangtse River, while north China was split into several kingdoms under different tribes. Yet the southern rulers continued to lead lives of wanton luxury. Thus while progress was made in methods of production thanks to the large number of northerners with superior technique and tools who moved south, the common people were still ground down by the nobles and great landowners. Conscript labour and military service were constantly exacted. Oppression was widespread and massacres a common occurrence. In both north China and south of the Yangtse men had no illusions. Their hatred for the ruling class and longing for better days found expression in incessant revolts, as well as in these stories of the supernatural. It is this that gives these tales their specific social content and realism.

During the Han dynasty shamanism was still commonly practised, and men lent a ready ear to the teaching of magicians and alchemists. Emperor Wu took a keen interest in the search for elixirs and Emperor Kuang-wu in oracles and divination. And the prevalence of such superstitions fostered the growth of these tales of the supernatural. By the end of the Han dynasty Taoism was widespread, and Buddhist ideas had begun to come in from India as communications with the west improved. Buddhism became a new force in Chinese civilization and contributed to the variety of these stories.

Since these stories developed under such historical conditions, although they give indirect expression to the people's feelings and wishes, they inevitably embody certain defects. Thus they are filled with superstition, animism, and ideas of divine retribution and the transmigration of the soul, while the feudal concepts of Confucian morality are strongly endorsed here. Marriages arranged by parents are considered quite normal, and acts of personal revenge are highly praised. While such views were a natural result of the social conditions of the time, we should point them out when introducing these stories so that the readers may distinguish between these feudal dregs and the genuine feelings and aspirations of the people, and understand the realism of these tales.

Many of these stories reveal clearly the people's hatred of oppression. "The Sword-Maker" tells how a swordmaker's son gave his life to avenge his father whom the king had killed. "Han Ping and His Wife" shows love which would not yield to temptations or threats. "The Dog from the Village Tavern" is something of a satire which, by hinting that a high official was a dog, expresses the general contempt for officials. Other tales deal with social problems of that period. In "Iron Mortar" a stepson takes revenge on the stepmother who has hounded him to death. The theme of "The King of Wu's Daughter" is freedom in marriage: the princess dies of a broken heart but her ghost meets her lover again. In fact, all the problems of the feudal family are raised in these ghost stories. Sometimes the message is clearly conveyed, at others it is implied, as in "The Powder Girl" and "The Lovelorn Spirit."

In certain stories the ghosts and devils represent the ugliness of the ruling class. Elsewhere they symbolize the people's indomitable spirit, or show the author's sympathy with suffering.

Anecdotes about real men form one important category in this ancient fiction. *Prince Tan's Revenge* is an early example of this, but the most famous collection of such anecdotes is the *New Anecdotes of Social Talk*.

Social Talk does not deal with the supernatural or with religion but reveals certain other aspects of feudal thought. It affirms the feudal way of life, feudal morality and aesthetics. It affirms deliberate escapism and abandonment, as well as such bad habits of the idle rich as gossip and the affectation of culture. At the same time, however, it gives us a fairly truthful picture of the ruling class at that time with its decadence and corruption, together with sketches of good characters.

These tales are not only rich in content, but have their merits also as literature. Though most of them deal with the supernatural, they appear intensely human. Ghosts and fairies talk and behave in a very natural way, with genuine feeling. Thus the fairy of Chinghsi Temple acts like any girl in love. These tales are remarkably compact, the development of the plot is skilfully handled, and the characterization is excellent. Hence these simple accounts are vivid and evocative. Some anecdotes in *Social Talk* consist of a few sentences only, yet are full of significance. The language of the time is concise to a high degree; and whether the theme is heroism, as in "The Serpent Sacrifice," or vengeance, as in "The Merchant's Revenge," the authors know how to hold the readers' interest.

For more than a thousand years the best of these tales have formed an important part of China's literary heritage and exercised a great influence on later fiction. This literary form persisted till after the eighteenth century. Indeed, the well-known *Tales of Liao-chai* by Pu Sungling is a continuation of this tradition. Many of these stories were also adapted by later writers. To name but a few examples: "The Cedar Pillow" inspired the Tang dynasty story *The Governor of the Southern Tributary State*; "Tung Yung and the Weaving Maid" is the theme today of local operas; "The Sword-Maker" was rewritten by Lu Hsun. Some folk tales of this period, like "The Haunted House" or "The Lady of the White Stream," are still widely popular. The modern versions may be more elaborate, but essentially they are the same.

In ancient China many types of writing were known as fiction (*hsiao shuo*). We have selected only those which have a story to tell, omitting accounts of distant lands, local products and customs, the sayings of famous men, or jokes.

An appendix gives a brief account of the various works from which these stories are chosen; but since in several cases the dates are uncertain, it is impossible to arrange them in strictly chronological order. We have, on the whole, put the ghost and fairy stories before the anecdotes of famous men.

To help foreign readers to visualize the life and society of that period in China, we have chosen as illustrations a number of reproductions of works of art dating from the third to the sixth century. Though these have no direct bearing on the tales, we hope they will supply something of the background and spirit of that age.

Our thanks are due to Mr. Wu Hsiao-ju, lecturer of the Department of Chinese Literature of Peking University, who rendered us great assistance in the selection of these stories.

July 1958

CONTENTS

A stone relief in a third century tomb showing an acrobatic display

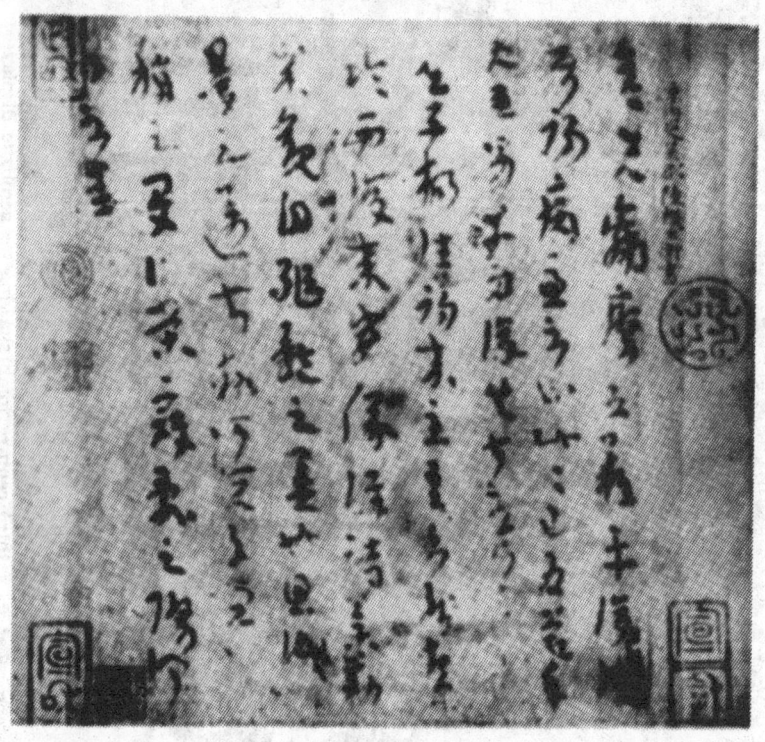

Calligraphy of the Tsin dynasty scholar Lu Chi (261-303)

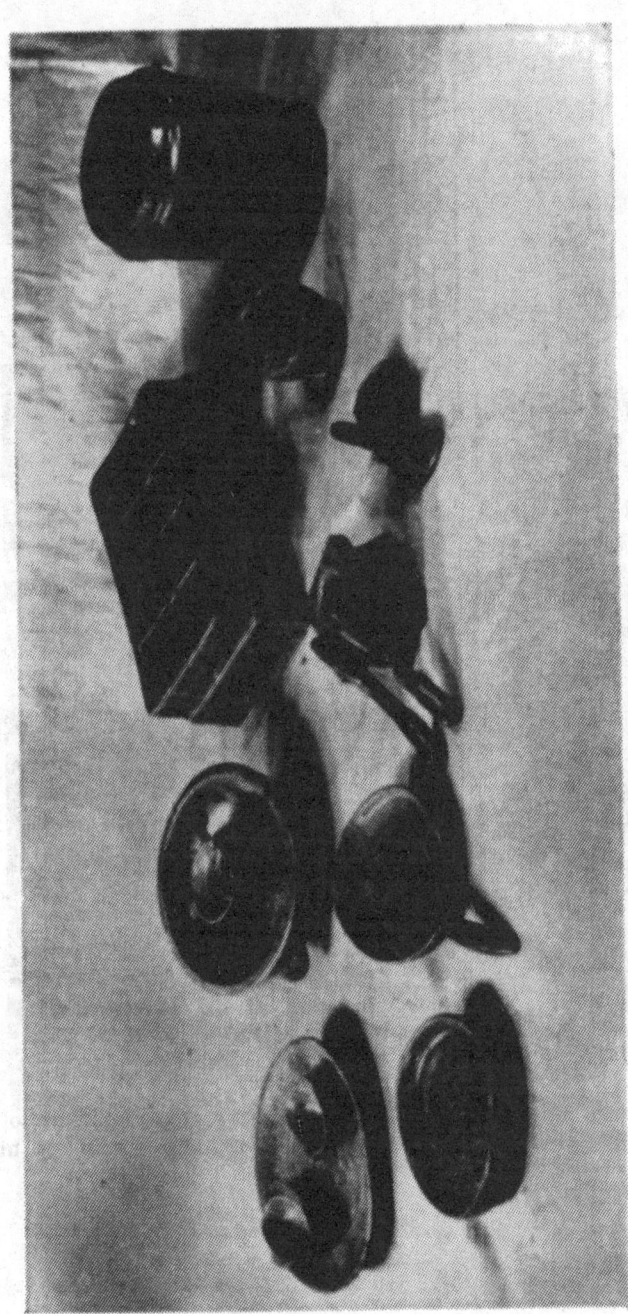

Pottery models of household utensils found in the tomb of Chou Chu, a Tsin dynasty general who died in 297

The stone unicorn-like animal in front of the sepulchre of
Hsiao Tao-sheng, fifth century founder of the kingdom of Chi

A procession of musicians shown in relief on a brick from the sixth century kingdom of Northern Wei

THE MAN WHO SOLD A GHOST

When Tsung Ting-po of Nanyang was young, he met a ghost one night as he was walking.

"Who are you?" he asked.

"A ghost, sir. Who are you?"

"A ghost like yourself," lied Tsung.

"Where are you going?"

"To the city."

"So am I."

They went on together for a mile or so.

"Walking is most exhausting. Why not carry each other in turn?" suggested the ghost.

"A good idea," agreed Tsung.

First the ghost carried him for some distance.

"How heavy you are!" said the ghost. "Are you really a spectre?"

"I am a new ghost," answered Tsung. "That is why I am heavier than usual."

Then he carried the ghost, who was no weight at all. And so they went on, changing several times.

"As I am a new ghost," said Tsung presently, "I don't know what we spectres are most afraid of."

"Being spat at by men — that is all."

They went on in company till they came to a stream. Tsung told the ghost to cross first, which it did without a sound. But Tsung made quite a splash.

"Why do you make such a noise?" inquired the ghost.

"I only died recently. I am not used to fording streams. You must excuse me."

As they approached the city, Tsung threw the ghost over his shoulder and held it tight. The ghost gave

1

a screech and begged to be put down, but Tsung would not listen and made straight for the market. When he set the ghost down it had turned into a goat. He promptly sold it, having first spat at it to prevent it changing its form again. Then he left, the richer by one thousand five hundred coins.

So the saying spread:

> Tsung Ting-po did better than most—
> He made money by selling a ghost.

THE SHRINE TO THE ANGRY BULL

In Wutu County stands the Shrine to the Angry Bull. They say this deity was a giant catalpa tree on the south hill. In the twenty-seventh year of his reign, Duke Wen of Chin sent men to fell this tree, but each time they gashed the trunk it healed again. Even when the duke sent forty men with axes, they could not cut it down. Tired out, they all went home except one man who was unable to leave because he had hurt his foot. He lay down under the tree, and there he heard two spirits talking.

Said one: "Have you not had enough of fighting?"

Said the other: "It is tedious, certainly."

"What if the duke goes on and on?"

"What harm can he do me?"

"Suppose he sends men in red to sprinkle ashes on you?"

At that the other was silent.

The wounded man reported this to the duke, who told his men to put on red clothes and sprinkle ashes on each cut they made. By this means the tree was felled. It changed into a bull which plunged into the stream. Because of this a shrine was erected here.

THE LOST HORSE

The city tribune, Pao Hsuan, was a native of Shangtang whose other name was Tzu-tu. As a young man he was on his way to the capital for an examination when he met a scholar travelling alone who had a pain in his chest. Pao alighted from his carriage to attend to him. But very soon the other died, not having disclosed his name, leaving a scroll of writing and ten silver pieces. Pao spent one piece of silver on the funeral, placed the rest under the dead man's head and spread the scroll over his body. After mourning he left him, saying:

"If your spirit is conscious after death, let your family know where you are. I have business and cannot stay with you any longer."

When Pao reached the capital a fine steed attached itself to him but would let no one else approach it. Returning home Pao lost his way, and went up to a nobleman's house, hoping they might put him up for the night. He asked for the master, and gave the slave his card. When the slave saw the horse, he hastened in to report to the nobleman:

"The stranger outside has stolen that steed you lost."

His master said: "Pao Hsuan is a well-known scholar of Shangtang. There must be some reason for this." He asked Pao: "How did you come by this horse which I lost the other year?"

Pao told him: "On my way to the capital I met a scholar who died on the road. . . ." He told the whole story from beginning to end. The nobleman was aghast.

"That was my son!" he cried.

He went to fetch the coffin, and upon opening it found the silver and scroll there just as Pao had said. Then the nobleman went to court to recommend Pao, and Pao's fame spread far and wide.

THE HAUNTED HOUSE

Chang Fen was a rich man of the principality of Wei. Suddenly falling into a decline, he sold his house to the Cheng family of Liyang. But after moving in, one after another they fell ill and died. Then they in turn sold the house to Ho Wen of Yeh.

One evening Ho sat with drawn sword on the beam in the main hall facing south. At the second watch, he saw a figure over ten feet high come in, dressed in a tall hat and yellow garment.

"Slender Waist!" called this apparition. "Why do I smell a living man?"

"There is no one here," was the answer.

Then another in a tall hat and green came in, and after him another in a tall hat and white. Both asked the same question and received the same answer.

When it was nearly dawn, Ho came down and called "Slender Waist!" as the others had.

"Who is the one in yellow?" he demanded.

"Gold," came the answer. "Under the west wall of the hall."

"Who is the one in green?"

"Copper, five paces from the well in front of the hall."

"Who is the one in white?"

"Silver, beneath the pillar in the north-east corner."

"And who are you?"

"A pestle under the stove."

At daybreak Ho dug where he had been told, and found five hundred catties of gold, five hundred catties of silver, and more than ten million copper coins. When he burned the pestle the house ceased to be haunted.

THE PRINCE OF SUIYANG'S DAUGHTER

The scholar Tan was still unmarried at forty, much to his distress. One night he was studying *The Book of Songs* at midnight when a girl of about sixteen came in. Her beauty and splendour had no equal on earth, and she offered to be his wife. She warned him, though:

"I am no ordinary woman. For three years you must not look at me by torchlight."

They married and had a son, and when the boy was two years old, Tan could contain his curiosity no longer. While his wife lay asleep he held a torch over her. From the waist up she was flesh like any other woman, but from the waist down she was nothing but dry bones! Just then his wife woke up.

"You have wronged me, husband!" she cried. "I was soon to have become a mortal. Why couldn't you wait for one more year instead of holding that torch over me?"

Tan made abject apologies.

"Now we must part for ever," she said in tears. "You must take good care of my son. If you are too poor to support yourself, come with me now and I shall give you a present."

He followed her into a splendid hall — a rare building richly furnished — where she gave him a robe made of pearls.

"You can live on this," she told him.

And she tore a strip from his gown.

Later Tan sold the robe to the prince of Suiyang for ten million coins. As soon as the prince set eyes on it, he said:

"That belonged to my daughter. This fellow must be a grave-robber."

He had Tan tried, and refused to believe his story. But upon inspecting the grave, they found it unbroken. And when they opened it, under the coffin lid they discovered the strip of Tan's garment. They perceived that his son resembled the princess too. So at last the prince was convinced. Summoning Tan, he returned him the robe and made him his son-in-law, while the child was recommended for a post in the palace guard.

WOMAN INTO CARP

A man of Pengcheng took a wife but had no liking for her, and started sleeping outside. After a month or more she asked:

"Why don't you come home?"

"Because you slip out every night," was his reply.

"I never have!" she declared.

Her husband was surprised.

"As you let your fancy wander, you have been bewitched," his wife told him. "Next time someone comes, seize hold of her and fetch a light to find out what creature it is."

Later on a strange woman came pretending to be his wife, but hesitated on the threshold and had to be pushed in. As soon as she was in bed the man seized her and asked:

"Why do you go out every night?"

"You are having an affair with that girl in the east house," was the answer. "You have made up this story of ghosts to excuse yourself."

Then he let her off and they slept together. In the middle of the night it came to him:

"I am bewitched — this is not my wife!"

He seized her and shouted for a torch. The woman shrank and shrivelled, and when he looked she was a carp two feet long.

THE RAT IN HUMAN DRESS

During the Cheng Shih period (240-248) Chou Nan, Prince of Chungshan, was the governor of Hsiangyi. One day a rat in human dress came out of its hole into his hall, and told him that on such-and-such a day in such-and-such a month he would die. Chou Nan made no reply, and the rat returned to its hole. When the day arrived, the rat came out again in an official cap and red dress.

"Chou Nan, you will die at noon," it said.

Again Chou Nan made no reply, and the rat went slowly back into its hole. Later it came out again and said:

"It is nearly noon."

It withdrew, but returned several times to repeat its warning. At the hour of noon the rat said:

"Chou Nan, if you will not answer, what can I say?"

It staggered and fell down dead, its clothes disappearing. Chou Nan bade an attendant bring him its body for examination. It looked like any ordinary rat.

TUNG YUNG AND THE WEAVING MAID

In the Han dynasty there lived a man of Chiencheng named Tung Yung. Having lost his mother as a child, he helped his father till the land and pull their cart. When his father died and he had no money for the funeral, he sold himself as a slave to pay for it. His master, knowing of his piety, gave him ten thousand coins and sent him off. After he had observed the three years' mourning, he went back to serve as a slave, and met a woman on the road who offered to be his wife. So they went on together.

His master told him: "That money was a gift."

But Tung replied: "Thanks to your help I was able to bury my father fittingly. Though I am low-born, I shall work hard to repay your kindness."

His master asked: "What can this woman do?"

Tung answered: "She can weave."

His master said: "In that case, let her just weave me a hundred rolls of silk."

Then Tung Yung's wife wove silk for this family, finishing her task in ten days. When she left she told Tung Yung:

"I am the Weaving Maid from Heaven. Because you are a filial son, the Heavenly Emperor ordered me to help you repay your debt."

Having said this she soared up into the air and disappeared.

THE JADE MAIDEN

Hsuan Chao was secretary in the provincial government of Chipei. During the Chiaping period (249-253) of the Wei dynasty, he dreamed that a goddess had come to his lonely bed.

"I am the Jade Maiden from Heaven," she announced. "A native of Tungchun named Cheng-kung, I lost my parents when I was a child. And the Heavenly Emperor, pitying my loneliness, has sent me to be your wife."

This dream was remarkably vivid, and Hsuan marvelled at her more than mortal beauty. When he awoke he longed for her as if she were close at hand. So three or four nights passed.

Then one day she came to visit him in person, riding in a curtained carriage with eight serving-maids dressed in embroidered silks, each lovely as a winged fairly. Though she told him her age was seventy, she looked like a girl of sixteen. In her carriage were a wine-pot and dishes — five pieces of pale green glassware. The food and wine were exquisite, and as she shared them with Hsuan she said to him:

"I am the Jade Maiden sent from Heaven to marry you — that is why I am here. It is not to repay former kindness, but because we were destined to be husband and wife. I cannot advance you, but neither will I harm you. You can ride with me in swift carriages or on good steeds, you can share with me food and drink from distant lands, and you will never want for clothes. Since I am immortal I cannot bear you a son; but I will not be jealous of other women, and you may still marry according to the custom."

12

Thus they lived as husband and wife, and she presented him with a poem which began:

High above fairy islands,
I drift over rocks and clouds;
The sacred herb grows without nourishment,
And its great virtue lasts to the end of time.
Immortals never descend to earth for nothing,
But to help men as fate decrees.
Accepting me will bring you prosperity,
Offending me will cause you calamity. . . .

There was more in the same vein, but since the poem came to over two hundred words we will not quote it in full. She also made notes on *The Book of Change*, giving explanations for the hexagrams and sayings. These commentaries were logically reasoned and as fit for divination as Yang Hsiung's *Tai Hsuan* or Hsueh's *Chung Ching*. Though Hsuan could not understand them fully, he used them as oracles to divine the future.

When Hsuan and this immortal had lived together for seven or eight years, his parents found him a wife. Then the Jade Maiden feasted and slept with him on certain days only, coming at night and leaving at dawn as swiftly as if on wings, and none but Hsuan could see her. Voices were heard when he was alone, and her presence was felt though she was invisible. Later prying friends questioned him, and learned his secret. Then the Jade Maiden took her leave.

"I am an immortal," she said. "I did not want my visits to you known. Since you have been careless enough to reveal my secret, I shall not come back again. We have loved each other for many years, and now that we must part how can I help grieving? But what must be must be. Take good care of yourself."

She bade her attendants bring wine and food, and took from a basket two sets of silk garments for him. She also gave him a poem. Then after a last embrace they

13

wept and parted. She mounted her carriage silently and left swiftly as the wind. For days Hsuan pined for her and nearly fell ill.

Five years later, official business took Hsuan to Loyang. He was travelling westward at the foot of Yu Mountain when he saw at a bend in the road a carriage like hers. When the carriage drew near, it proved indeed to belong to the Jade Maiden. She parted the curtains and they greeted each other with mingled joy and sorrow. Then she turned back and rode with him to Loyang, where they lived together again and renewed their love. They were still together in the Taikang period (28-289) of the Tsin dynasty, though she did not come every day. Only on the third of the third month, the fifth of the fifth month, the seventh of the seventh month, the ninth of the ninth month, and the first and fifteenth of the tenth month would she spend the night with him, leaving at dawn. Inspired by this story, the scholar Chang Hua wrote a poem called *The Fairy Maid*.

THE LORD OF TAISHAN

Hu-mu Pan, whose other name was Chi-yu, was a native of Taishan. One day in the forest at the foot of the mountain he met a red-coated horseman, who called to him:

"The Lord of Taishan requests your company."

Taken aback, Hu-mu hesitated to reply. But when another horseman came to call him, he followed them several dozen yards till they bade him close his eyes. Then he saw a magnificent palace. He went in to pay his respects to the god, who feasted him and said:

"My sole motive in asking to see you was to beg you to take a letter to my son-in-law."

"Where is your daughter's palace?" inquired Hu-mu.

"She is the River God's wife."

"I shall certainly take your letter, but how can I reach her?"

"Stop your boat in midstream and call her maid. Someone will come for the letter."

Then Hu-mu took his leave. Again the horsemen bade him close his eyes, and soon he found himself on the same path as before. He went west and did as the god had said. When he called the River God's maid, a woman emerged, took the letter and disappeared into the river. She appeared again to say:

"The River God wishes to meet you."

And she told him to close his eyes. Then Hu-mu paid his respects to the River God, who entertained him to a sumptuous feast and showed him great courtesy. When he was leaving the god said to him:

"I am grateful to you for coming all this way with the letter, but I do not know what to give you."

Then he told his followers to fetch his silk sandals as a gift for Hu-mu. Upon leaving him, Hu-mu found himself suddenly in his boat. He went on to Changan and returned after a year. When he reached the mountain he did not dare pass by without a word. He knocked on a tree, announcing himself, and reported that he brought news from the capital. The same horsemen came out and led him as before to the god, to whom he presented a letter. The Lord of Taishan bade him good speed and promised to repay his kindness. Then Hu-mu went to the privy, where he found his father in chains with some other prisoners who were doing hard labour there. Hu-mu went forward and bowed, shedding tears.

"How did you come to this, sir?"

His father replied: "Alas! After my death I was sentenced to penal servitude for three years. I have just served two of them. The work is unbearably hard. I hear you are a friend of the Lord of Taishan. I wish you would put in a word to get me off. I would like to go back to my village."

Then Hu-mu kowtowed to the god and pleaded for his father. The Lord of Taishan said:

"It is not that I grudge you anything. But dead and living have different ways and should not mingle."

Hu-mu pleaded again and again, and did not leave until the lord consented. After he had been home for more than a year, however, most of his children died, and in great alarm he went back to Taishan. He knocked on the tree and asked to see the god, and the same horsemen conducted him there.

"Since I left you to return home nearly all my sons have died," lamented Hu-mu. "For fear these misfortunes may continue, I have come to report this and beg you to have pity."

The god clapped his hands and laughed.

"What did I tell you? Living and dead have different ways and should not be near each other."

16

He sent men to summon Hu-mu's father. Soon the old man came to the court. The Lord of Taishan said:

"Since you asked to go back to your village, you should have rendered assistance to your descendants. How is it that all these children died?"

Hu-mu's father replied: "Having been away from my native district so long I was overjoyed to be back. When I had enough wine and food, I longed to have my grandsons with me — so I summoned them."

The god ordered another spirit to take his place, and Hu-mu's father left in tears. After Hu-mu's return all his children remained safe and sound.

THE LORD OF LUSHAN

Chang Pu, whose other name was Kung-chih and whose native place is not known, served as governor of Wu. On his way back to the capital from this post he passed Lushan, and his children visited the temple on the mountain. Their maid pointed to an image and teased Chang's daughter:

"We shall marry you to this god!"

That night Chang's wife dreamed that the Lord of Lushan had come with betrothal gifts.

"My son is a worthless fellow. We are grateful to you for choosing him as your son-in-law. I have brought these gifts to express my thanks."

The wife woke up, amazed. Told by the maid what had happened at the temple, she implored her husband to set off again at once. In midstream their boat stopped short, and terror seized them all. They threw their possessions overboard, but still the boat would not move. Then some suggested that if the daughter were thrown into the Yangtse the vessel would proceed.

"The god's wishes are clear," they said. "Why sacrifice the whole household for one child?"

But Chang said: "I cannot bear to watch it."

He told his wife to throw the girl into the water, while he himself lay down. The girl's mother substituted the daughter of Chang's dead brother for their own. She placed a mat on the water and made her sit on it. Thereupon the boat moved off. When Chang saw his daughter still aboard he was very angry.

"How can I face the world again?" he cried.

So he threw his own child into the water too.

After they had crossed the river, he saw the two girls with an officer on the bank.

"I am the Lord of Lushan's secretary," said the officer. "He sends you his thanks and says that he knows the daughters of men should not marry immortals. He is so impressed by your loyalty to your brother that he has sent both girls back."

Later Chang asked the girls what had happened. They had simply seen fine buildings, officers and men, but had never known that they were under the water.

SISTER TING

Ting, a girl of sixteen from Tanyang, married Hsieh of Chuanchiao south of the Huai River. Her mother-in-law was a shrew, and unless the girl finished her tasks by a certain time she was cruelly whipped or beaten. On the ninth day of the ninth month that year, Ting hanged herself. Her spirit haunted men, and through the witch-doctors she announced:

"Because I pity young wives who have no respite from their toil, let them rest on the ninth day of the ninth month. No work should be done that day."

She also appeared in human form in a green dress, attended by a maid. She went to Niuchu Ford to find someone to ferry her across the river. When she asked two men who were fishing to take her on their boat, they jeered at her.

"Be our wife, and we'll row you across!"

"I thought you were decent folk, but I see you are fools," she retorted. "If you are men, you will perish in the mud. If you are ghosts, you will vanish in the water."

Then she went to the reedy shore. Soon an old man arrived with a boat laden with hay, and she asked him to take her across.

The old man said: "My boat has no awning. How can you go uncovered? This is no way for a lady to travel."

But she said it did not matter; so the old man removed half the hay from his boat, and ferried her slowly across. When she reached the south bank and was leaving, she told him:

"I am no living woman but a spirit. I could have crossed the stream myself, but I wanted my presence known. It was very good of you to leave your load to ferry me across. I am most grateful and shall repay your kindness. If you go back now, you will see a strange sight and find something to your advantage."

The old man said: "I'm afraid you had an uncomfortable crossing — how can I let you thank me?"

Upon returning to the west bank, he discovered two men lying face down in the water. A little further on he found thousands of fish leaping ashore, blown by the wind. So the old man abandoned his hay and went back with a load of fish. Ting's ghost returned to Tanyang, and everyone south of the Yangtse called her Sister Ting. The ninth day of the ninth month is a holiday for women, who do no work that day. Even now there are shrines far and wide to Sister Ting.

THE SWORD-MAKER

Because Kanchiang Moya took three years to forge a pair of swords for the king of Chu, the king was angry and determined to kill him. One sword was male, the other female. Kanchiang's wife was about to give birth, and her husband told her:

"I have taken three years to make these swords for the king. Now he is angry. When I go there he will kill me. If you give birth to a son, once he is grown tell him that if he goes out and faces the south hill he will see a pine growing on a stone with a sword in its back."

Then Kanchiang took the female sword to the king. The king flew into a rage, for he knew that there were two swords, one male and one female, and the female sword was there but not the male. In a passion he killed the sword-maker.

Kanchiang's son was named Chih. When he grew up he asked his mother:

"Where is my father?"

She told him:

"Your father took three years to make a pair of swords for the king of Chu. The king was angry and killed him. But before he left home he bade me tell you that if you go out and face the south hill, you will find a pine growing on a stone with a sword in its back."

The son went out and faced south, but he saw no hill. All he saw was a pine-wood pillar on a stone base in front of the hall. Cutting it open with his axe, he found the sword. Then day and night he thirsted for revenge.

The king saw in a dream a boy with a brow one foot across who wanted to take revenge on him. He offered a thousand gold pieces for his head. And when Chih heard this he fled lamenting to the mountains. There a stranger accosted him.

"You are young," he said. "Why should you wail so bitterly?"

"I am the son of Kanchiang Moya. The king of Chu killed my father. I want revenge."

"I hear the king has offered a thousand gold pieces for your head. Give me your head and your sword, and I will avenge you."

"Very well," agreed the boy.

Then he killed himself and, standing upright, presented his head and the sword with both hands to the other.

"I shall not let you down," promised the stranger.

Then the boy's body fell to the ground.

The stranger took the head to the king, who was very pleased.

"This is the head of a brave man," said the stranger. "You should boil it in a seething cauldron."

The king did as he said. But even after three days and three nights the head would not melt away. It leaped out of the boiling water and glared in anger.

"This boy's head will not melt," said the stranger, "until Your Majesty comes to look at it."

When the king walked up, the stranger drew the sword and struck his head off into the boiling water. He then cut off his own head, which fell into the cauldron too, and all three heads melted and intermingled. So the flesh and the soup were divided into three portions and buried in a place called the Grave of the Three Kings. This grave is in the county of Yichun north of Junan.

HAN PING AND HIS WIFE

Han Ping, steward to Prince Kang of Sung, married a beautiful daughter of the Ho family. But the prince stole her from him. When Han protested, he was imprisoned and sentenced to hard labour on the city wall. His wife wrote him a secret message:

> Rain, ceaseless rain,
> Wide the river, deep the flood,
> Yet sunrise is in my heart.

This letter fell into the hands of the prince, who showed it to his followers, but none could make out its meaning until the minister Su Ho said:

"The first line means that she longs for him continuously, the second that they have no way of meeting, the third that she intends to take her life."

Then Han Ping killed himself.

His wife secretly tore her clothes, and when the prince went up the tower with her, she threw herself from the top. His followers tried to seize her, but her clothes came away in their hands and she was dashed to death. On her belt she had left this message:

"Your Highness wished me to live, but your servant chose to die. Please bury me with Han Ping."

The prince was angry and refused her request, ordering the local people to bury her in a separate grave.

"You speak of your undying love," sneered the prince. "If you can make these tombs come together, I will not stand in your way."

Then within one day two great catalpa trees sprang up above the two graves. In ten days they grew to an enormous size. Their branches inclined towards each other, their roots intertwined beneath the soil, and their twigs interlaced above. And two love birds, one male and one female, stayed on these trees, not departing morning or night. They billed and cooed plaintively, and uttered heart-rending cries. The people of Sung lamented the lovers' death and called these trees "The Trees of Love." The southerners say these birds are the spirits of Han Ping and his wife. In Suiyang today there is a town named Hanping, and men still sing of the lovers.

TWO FRIENDS

During the Han dynasty a man named Fan Shih, whose other name was Chu-ching, lived in Chinhsiang County in Shanyang. He was devoted to Chang Shao of Junan, whose other name was Yuan-po. Both men studied in the Imperial Academy, and when they left to go home Fan told Chang:

"Two years from now I shall call on your family."

So they fixed upon a date. When the time appointed drew near, Chang asked his mother to prepare for a guest.

His mother said: "You have not seen him for two years and he is far away. How can you believe him so implicitly?"

"Fan can be trusted. He never breaks his word."

"In that case, I shall prepare wine for you."

On the appointed day Fan came. He ascended the hall and greeted them, drinking wine and enjoying their company before leaving. Later Chang fell ill and his disease proved mortal. Tao Chun-chang and Yin Tzu-cheng, two friends from the same district, tended him day and night. But on his death bed he sighed:

"Would I could see my best friend once again!"

Yin protested: "We have nursed you as well as we could. What better friend do you have?"

"You are my friends in life," replied Chang. "But Fan of Shanyang is my friend even in death."

Then he expired. Fan saw Chang in a dream, in sandals and a dark hat with tassels, calling out that he had died on such-and-such a day and would be buried on such-and-such a day.

"Chu-ching!" he cried. "I shall remain for ever in the nether regions. You have not forgotten me, but when shall we meet again?"

When Fan awoke he sighed and shed tears. Then, putting on mourning, he went on the day appointed to the funeral. The ceremony started before he arrived; but when the procession reached the burial ground the coffin could not be moved forward. Chang's mother clapped her hand on it and asked:

"Are you expecting something?"

So they waited for a little. Presently they saw Fan in a white carriage drawn by white horses. He was weeping. Seeing him in the distance, Chang's mother said:

"This must be Fan Chu-ching."

When Fan arrived, he clasped the coffin and cried:

"Go now! We are separated by death and must go our different ways. Farewell!"

All the thousand mourners at the funeral shed tears. Then Fan took the rope fastening the coffin, and it moved forward. Fan stayed by the grave and planted trees beside it before he left.

THE DOG CALLED PAN HU

In the time of King Kao-hsin[1] an old woman in the palace had a pain in her ear, and the physician who treated her removed a worm as large as a cocoon. The woman having left, the worm was placed in a gourd and covered with a plate. It changed into a mottled dog, which was given the name Pan Hu and kept in the palace.

At that time the Wu barbarians were strong and often invaded the king's territory; and the generals sent against them could not defeat them. So the king offered a thousand pounds of gold, a fief of ten thousand households, and the hand of his youngest daughter to whomsoever should bring him the head of the chief of Wu. Then Pan Hu came to the palace with a human head in its mouth, and the king saw this was the head of the enemy chieftain. He was at a loss what to do.

His ministers said: "Pan Hu is a beast. We cannot give a dog gold and a fief, let alone a wife. Though it has done this, no reward need be given."

But the king's youngest daughter, hearing this, protested to her father:

"Your Majesty promised to give me away in marriage and the dog has brought you this, ridding our state of a danger. This must be owing to the will of Heaven, not to the dog's intelligence. Kings and conquerors must keep their word. You cannot break a promise made to the people in order to save one girl, for that would bring trouble on our land."

---

[1] According to legend, the great-grandson of the Yellow Emperor.

The king had perforce to agree, and he ordered her to accompany Pan Hu. Then Pan Hu took the princess to the southern hill which was overgrown with trees and brambles, with no human habitation. She took off her royal clothes and dressed as a slave to go with the dog to a valley in the mountain, where they stayed in a rocky cave. The king missed his daughter sadly, and sent men in search of her. But whenever they went out there was a storm: the hills quaked and were covered with dark clouds which made it impossible for them to find her.

Three years passed, and she gave birth to six boys and six girls. After Pan Hu died the boys and girls married each other. They made clothes of the bark of trees and dyed them with seeds, for they loved colourful garments; and they all had tails. Later their mother went back and told the king what had happened. The king sent envoys to fetch these children, and this time there was no storm. Their clothes were garish and their speech barbaric. They squatted to eat and drink, loved mountains and hated cities. So to please them the king gave them mountainous and marshy country, and they were called the *Man* barbarians.

HORSE INTO SILKWORM

It is said that in very ancient times a man made a long journey, leaving only his daughter at home with a stallion in her care. She was so lonely that she longed for her father, and one day she said jokingly to the horse:

"If you bring my father home, I will marry you!"

At once the horse broke its tether and galloped off to where her father was. Surprised and pleased to see it, he jumped into the saddle. The stallion kept whinnying sadly, gazing back in the direction from which it had come.

"There must be some reason for this," thought the man. "Can there have been an accident at home?"

Immediately he rode back. And because the beast had shown such intelligence he treated it well, giving it extra fodder. The horse would not eat, however, but when it saw the girl pass in or out it would rear up in excitement — this happened more than once. The father was puzzled and secretly questioned his daughter, who told him what must be the cause.

"Hush!" he said. "You will disgrace our family. You had better not leave the house for the time being."

He took a crossbow and killed the horse, then flayed it and hung its hide in the courtyard.

When the man left home again, the girl and a neighbour's daughter started playing near the hide. The girl kicked it, saying:

"You beast! How dare you think of marrying a girl? Shot and flayed — you brought it on yourself!"

While she was speaking the hide reared up, wrapped itself around her and made off. The neighbour's daughter was too afraid to try to rescue her. Instead she ran to tell her father. When he came and searched for them they had disappeared, but a few days later they were found on a great tree. The girl and the hide had been changed into a silkworm which was spinning silk on the tree — spinning a large, thick cocoon the like of which had never been seen before. The neighbouring women, who kept these cocoons, made several times their former profit. So the tree was named *sang* or mulberry, which means "lost."[1] Since then everyone has cultivated it, and this is the silkworm which we have today.

---

[1] 桑 *sang* for mulberry has the same sound as 喪 *sang* meaning "lost."

THE OLD MAN IN THE HOUSE

During the Chienan period (196-219) in the reign of Emperor Hsien Ti of Han, there were strange happenings in a house in Tungchun. Pots and crockery clattered in an empty room as if someone were knocking them; dishes disappeared before men's eyes, and when the hens laid eggs these vanished too. This went on for several years, until the whole household was worried. They prepared a number of good dishes, covered them and put them in a certain room while they hid behind a door to watch. When the Thing came again and the same noises were heard, they immediately closed the door and searched the room — but nothing could they find. They struck out with sticks in the dark until after some time, in one corner of the room, they hit something.

"Help! Help!" a voice groaned. "I am dying!"

They opened the door and found an old man more than a hundred years old. His speech was odd and he looked half man half beast. When they asked where he came from they discovered that his home was not many miles away. The old man's relatives had lost him for more than ten years, and were torn between grief and joy at finding him. After another year they lost him again. Similar strange happenings were reported in the principality of Chenliu, and it was generally believed that this must be due to the same old man.

THE OLD MAN AND THE DEVILS

Chin Chu-po of the principality of Langya was sixty. One night after drinking, as he passed Pengshan Temple, he saw his two grandsons coming towards him. They took his arms and helped him along for about a hundred paces. Then they seized him by the neck and threw him to the ground.

"Old slave!" they swore. "You beat us up the other day, so today we are going to kill you."

Remembering that he had indeed beaten the boys some days ago, he pretended to be dead, and they left him there. When he got home he decided to punish them. Shocked and distressed they apologized to him.

"How could your own grandsons do such a thing?" they protested. "Those must have been devils. Please make another test."

He realized they were right.

A few days later the old man pretended to be drunk and walked past the temple again. Once more the two devils came to take his arms, and this time he seized them so that they could not escape. Reaching home, he put both devils on the fire, until their backs and bellies were scorched and cracked. He left them in the courtyard, and that night they escaped. Sorry that he had not killed them, about a month later the old man pretended to be drunk and went out at night again, taking a sword, unknown to his family. When he did not come back though it was very late, his grandsons feared the devils had caught him again. They went to look for him. And this time the old man hacked his own grandsons to death.

THE KING OF WU'S DAUGHTER

Fu Chai, the king of Wu, had a gifted and beautiful daughter of eighteen named Tzu Yu, who fell in love with a learned youth of nineteen, Han Chung. They exchanged secret messages and she promised to marry him. When Han went north to study he asked his parents to arrange the match; but the king refused in great anger. Then the princess died of a broken heart and was buried outside the West Gate.

Three years later Han returned and questioned his parents.

"The king flew into a rage and the princess died of a broken heart," they told him. "Now she is in her grave."

At that Han wept bitterly. He prepared a sacrifice to mourn for her. Then the princess appeared from her grave and said with tears:

"When you left you asked your parents to approach my father, and we thought our wish would surely be granted. But alas! fate was against us."

With a sidelong glance, she hung her head and sang:

> Crows were on the southern hill,
> Nets upon the north were spread;
> Traps were laid, but laid in vain,
> Far away the birds have fled.
> Fain would I have followed you
> But obstructions barred the way;
> Falling ill of grief I died,
> Under yellow earth I lay;
> Pity my unhappy fate,
> Doomed to weep day after day!

Phoenix is the chief and queen
Whom each lesser fowl reveres;
Phoenix, when she lost her mate,
Wept and mourned for three whole years.
Phoenix could not find a mate
Though bright songsters filled the skies;
So despite my humble looks,
I appear before your eyes;
And though torn so far apart,
Still you keep me in your heart.

After this song she sobbed bitterly, unable to control her grief, and begged Han to accompany her into the grave.

"Dead and living must go different ways," said Han. "I fear that would hardly be fitting. I had better not."

"I know that dead and living go different ways," she replied. "But once we part we shall never meet again. Are you afraid that now I am a ghost I will harm you? I am completely sincere — why don't you trust me?"

Touched by her words, Han saw her back. In the grave they feasted for three days and three nights, and completed the rites of marriage. When he was leaving she gave him a pearl one inch across.

"My reputation was ruined and I never attained my heart's desire," she sighed. "What more is there to say? Take good care of yourself, and if you pass the palace, pay my respects to the king."

When Han left the grave he went to the king and told him what had happened. Fu Chai flew into a passion.

"My daughter is dead!" he exclaimed. "This fellow is lying to dishonour the dead. He is simply a grave-robber who has stolen this pearl and trumped up this story of a ghost. Arrest him at once!"

But the young man escaped and went back to the grave where he reported this to the princess.

"Don't worry," she said. "I shall speak to the king myself."

Then she appeared to her father as he was dressing. Joy, sorrow and amazement overcame him.

"What brings you back to life?" he demanded.

"When the young scholar Han Chung asked for my hand, you refused him," she replied, kneeling. "Having lost my good name and broken faith, I died. Recently he came back from far away, and hearing that I was dead he prepared a sacrifice to mourn at my grave. I was so touched by his loyalty that I appeared to him and gave him that pearl. He is no grave-robber. Please don't punish him."

When the queen heard this she came out to embrace her child. But the princess vanished like a puff of smoke.

MARRIED TO A GHOST

Lu Chung was a native of the principality of Fanyang. Thirty *li* west of his house was the graveyard of the Tsui family, one of whom had held office as imperial custodian. The day before the winter solstice when Lu was twenty, he went out in a westerly direction to hunt. He sighted a deer and pierced it with an arrow, but after falling it struggled up again. Then Lu gave chase and pursued it for some distance till suddenly, a few hundred yards to the north, he saw a large, tiled mansion resembling a government office. The deer had disappeared. The guard at the gate called out at his approach.

"Whose house is this?" asked Lu.

"The house of the imperial custodian."

"I am too shabby to call on him," said Lu.

Someone came out with an armful of new clothes and a new hat.

"Our master presents you with these," he announced.

Lu changed his clothes and went in to see the imperial custodian, to whom he introduced himself. After they had drunk and eaten several courses, his host said to Lu:

"Your father recently honoured our humble house by writing to ask for my daughter's hand for you. This is why I invited you in."

He showed Lu the letter. And though Lu had been a child when his father died, he could recognize the writing. With tears in his eyes he consented. Then the imperial custodian sent a message to the inner chambers that Lu Chung had arrived and his daughter should dress for her wedding. He bade Lu go to the east chamber.

By dusk word came from within that the girl was ready. When Lu entered the east chamber, she had alighted from her carriage. They stood on the carpet and bowed together, after which Lu stayed the customary three days. Then Tsui said to him:

"You may go home now. I fancy my daughter has conceived. If she gives birth to a son, rest assured we will send him to you. If to a daughter, we will keep her ourselves."

He ordered his men to harness the carriage for Lu, who took his leave and went out. The imperial custodian saw him to the middle gate where they shook hands and shed tears. Outside the gate, Lu saw an ox-cart with a driver in blue, and found his old clothes as well as his bow and arrows. Then a man was sent out with a suit of clothes which he gave to Lu with this message from his master: "We have just become related by marriage, and are very sorry that you are leaving so soon. Please accept this suit of clothes and bedding."

Lu mounted the cart which travelled as swiftly as lightning. In no time he was home. When his relatives saw him, they did not know whether to be glad or sorry. The knowledge that Tsui the imperial custodian was dead and that Lu had been in his grave made them rather uneasy.

Four years later, on the third day of the third month, Lu was strolling by the stream when he observed two carts drawn by oxen approach through the water. As they neared the bank, all those who were with him saw them. Lu opened the door at the back of the first cart and found Tsui's daughter with a three-year-old boy. He was overjoyed to see her, and wanted to take her hand. But she pointed at the cart behind.

"You had better see my father first!"

So he greeted the imperial custodian. The girl gave the baby to Lu, and presented him with a golden bowl and a poem which read as follows:

How beautiful and bright
The glorious herb divine;
Which shines at the appointed hour
With splendour strange and fine.

But'ere the herb can bloom
'Tis killed by summer frost;
Its grace destroyed for ever more,
Its splendid beauty lost.

Who knows the will of Heaven?
A stranger seeks our gate —
We meet but all too soon must part,
For men are rulled by fate.

What gift can I bestow?
This bowl I give my son;
And now we part for ever more,
Our love is past and done!

As soon as Lu took the child, the bowl and the poem, the two carts disappeared. When he carried the small boy home, everyone feared it must be a ghost and spat at it from a distance, but the child remained unchanged.

"Who is your father?" they asked.

It ran straight into Lu's arms.

At first all were amazed and felt forebodings; but when they read the poem they knew there was much mysterious traffic between the living and the dead.

Later Lu drove to the market to sell the bowl. He asked a very high price, for actually what he wanted was not to sell it but to find someone to identify it. An old woman slave recognized it, and went to tell her mistress:

"In the market I saw a man in a cart selling that bowl which was in Miss Tsui's coffin."

Her mistress was the girl's aunt. She sent her son to look at the bowl, and when he found that what the slave said was true he went to Lu's cart and introduced himself.

"One of my aunts married the imperial custodian and had a daughter," he said. "The girl died before her marriage, and my mother in her grief presented a golden bowl to put in the coffin. Can you tell me how you came by this bowl?"

Lu told him the story, at which the young man was moved. He took the bowl back to his mother, who asked to see the dead girl's son. All the Tsui clansmen assembled; and when they found that the child looked like one of themselves yet resembled Lu as well, they believed him.

"My niece was born at the end of the third month," said the aunt. "Her father said, 'The spring is warm and we hope the infant will prosper, so let us name her Wen-hsiu (warm and prosperous).' The name sounded like 'wedded in the grave.' That was surely an omen."

The boy grew into a talented man, and became a provincial governor with a two-thousand-bushel salary. All his descendants to this day have held official posts, while one, Lu Chih, was famed throughout the empire.

THE YOUNG MAN ON THE TREE

During the reign of Sun Hao of the Wu dynasty, Chu Tan, whose other name was Yung-chang, was promoted from the post of civil officer of Huainan to the governorship of Chienan. His secretary's wife was possessed by an evil spirit. At first her husband suspected her of playing him false. One day, therefore, after pretending to leave the house, he spied on her through a hole in the wall. He saw his wife weaving at her loom and holding a laughing conversation with someone some distance away on the mulberry tree. In this tree the secretary observed a youth of about fifteen in a black suit and black cap. Thinking this must be a messenger, he shot at him with his crossbow, whereupon the lad changed into a cicada as large as a winnowing fan and flew off. At the same time the wife exclaimed:

"Ah! Someone has shot you!"

The secretary was amazed. Some time later he saw two boys talking together on the road. One said:

"Why haven't I seen you for so long?"

The other was the lad who had been on the tree. He answered:

"I was unlucky enough to be shot, and it took me a long time to recover."

"How are you now?" asked the first.

"I treated my wound with some ointment from the beam in Governor Chu's house," was the reply. "Now I am better."

The secretary asked the governor:

"Do you know someone has been stealing your ointment?"

"Impossible," said the governor. "My ointment has been on the beam all this time."

The secretary said: "No. You had better look."

The governor did not believe him, and when he looked he found the seal unbroken.

"That fellow is talking nonsense!" he declared. "The ointment is untouched."

But the secretary insisted: "Open the packet."

Then the governor found the ointment inside half gone, and noticed the marks of nails. He was shocked, and asked for an explanation. Then his secretary related the whole story.

THE GHOST MET AT NIGHT

During the Huangchu period of the Wei dynasty, a man was riding at night through Tunchiu when he saw on the road a creature the size of a rabbit with eyes like two round mirrors. This thing leaped up and down in front of his horse so that it could not go on. And when the rider fell to the ground in fright, the apparition tried to catch him. The man fainted away with terror. By and by he came to himself, and found the monster gone. He remounted and rode on for several miles till he met another traveller. After exchanging greetings he told the stranger his story, saying how delighted he was to have company.

The other said: "I was travelling alone, and am very glad to have a companion on the road. Since you are mounted and can go faster, you had better lead the way and let me follow."

So they went on.

Presently the stranger asked: "What did that apparition look like to frighten you so?"

He answered: "It was the size of a rabbit, with eyes like two round mirrors — a fearful sight!"

The other said: "Look at me!"

The man turned his head. His companion had changed into the monster! This apparition leaped on to the horse, and the rider fell to the ground and fainted away. His family was surprised when the horse returned alone. Going in search of him, they discovered him by the roadside. He did not regain consciousness till the next day, when he told them all that had happened.

THE BRINDLED FOX AT THE
ANCIENT TOMB

Chang Hua, whose other name was Mao-hsien, served as chief minister under Emperor Huei of the Tsin dynasty. At that time in front of the tomb of King Chao of Yen there lived a very ancient brindled fox, able to assume other forms. One day it changed itself into a scholar in order to call on Chang Hua. But first it consulted the wooden pillar in front of the tomb.

"With my ability can I present myself to the chief minister in this form?"

"With your subtle understanding there is nothing you cannot do," replied the pillar. "But Chang Hua is so wise that you may find it hard to deceive him. Then you will be insulted and not allowed to return. Not only will you lose your chance of immortality but I shall suffer too."

The fox would not listen, however. It sent in its card to Chang Hua. And when Chang Hua saw this debonair young scholar with his jade-white complexion and graceful, charming manner, he showed him great respect. They talked of literature, arguing about form and substance, and Chang Hua learned much hitherto unknown to him. Then they discussed history and philosophy, the hidden meaning of Lao Tzu and Chuang Tzu, the finer points of *The Book of Songs,* the ten sages, the three virtues, the eight schools of Confucianism, the five types of ceremony — and Chang Hua was worsted in every argument. He sighed and said:

"There can be no such youth as this in the world! This is either a spirit or a fox."

He detained the young man under guard. The scholar protested:

"You should honour talent, noble sir, and show tolerance, commending the good and displaying modesty. Why take offence if others are learned? Is this in accordance with Mo Tzu's principle of Universal Love?"

He asked permission to leave. But Chang Hua's guards would not let him pass the gate.

"You have armed guards and cavalry at the gate," said the scholar. "Evidently you suspect me. I fear all men will take care to hold their tongues in future, and those in search of knowledge will pass by your door. I find this most deplorable, noble sir!"

Chang Hua made no reply, but ordered his men to keep a strict watch. The magistrate of Fengcheng at that time was Lei Huan, whose other name was Kungchang, a man of great erudition. Now he called on Chang Hua, who told him of this scholar.

"If you suspect him," said Lei, "why not try him with a hound?"

Then a hound was brought to test him, but the scholar did not change colour.

"I am a man of talent," he protested, "yet you take me for a monster and confront me with a dog. You may try ten thousand tricks, but you cannot harm me!"

When Chang Hua heard this he grew even more enraged.

"Without any doubt this is a monster," he said. "I have heard that only ogres a few hundred years old are afraid of dogs, not monsters who have lived nearly a thousand years. But if you shine a torch made from wood a thousand years old on them, they appear in their true form."

"Where can we get such wonderful wood a thousand years old?" asked Lei.

"They say the wooden pillar in front of the tomb of

45

King Chao of Yen is a thousand years old," replied Chang Hua.

He sent a man to cut it down. As the man approached the place, a boy in dark clothes appeared and asked:

"What brings you here?"

"A young man has called on Minister Chang," was the answer. "He is so brilliant and eloquent that the minister suspects he is a monster. I have been sent to get that pillar to burn by him."

"The old fox is a fool!" cried the boy. "He would not listen to me, and now I am involved in his trouble. There is no escape!"

With a cry of anguish he vanished into thin air. When the man cut down the pillar, blood flowed from it. Then the wood was carried back and set aflame to cast its light on the scholar, who was at once revealed as a brindled fox.

"If these two creatures had not met me," said Chang Hua, "after a thousand years we could never have caught them!"

He had the fox boiled in a cauldron.

THE OLD CAT

During the Tsin dynasty a man of Wuhsing had two sons. He often cursed, chased or beat them when they were at work in the fields. The two young men told their mother, who questioned her husband. Shocked to realize that some spirit was taking his form, he advised his sons to draw their swords and kill it. Then the spirit ceased to appear.

The father, worried lest his sons be overpowered by the monster, went to the fields himself. But the sons, mistaking him for the apparition, killed him and buried him. Then the spirit went to their home in their father's form, and told the family that his sons had killed the monster. And the young men, coming back in the evening, congratulated themselves. This went on for over a year without their realizing the truth, until a priest passed the house and said to the sons:

"Your father has an evil aura."

When the sons told their father this, he was very angry. The sons came out to send the priest away; but he walked in chanting his incantations, and the father changed into an old cat which crawled under the bed. After catching the cat and killing it, they knew that it was their own father they had killed before. So now they gave him a fresh funeral. Then one son took his own life. The other died of anger and remorse.

CATCHING THE OLD FOX

There was a station-house in the west suburb of Nanyang in which no one could live, for strange sights were seen there. Sung Ta-hsien of that district was an upright man. One night he climbed to the second floor of that house and sat there playing his lyre — he had come unarmed. At midnight a ghost appeared and accosted him. This ghost had glittering eyes, sharp fangs and a fearful appearance, but Sung went on playing his lyre as if nothing had happened. The ghost went off to the market to return with a dead man's head.

"Won't you sleep a while?" it asked Sung, and tossed him the head.

"Very good," said Sung. "I have no pillow. This is just what I need."

Then the ghost went off again. By and by it came back.

"Would you like to wrestle with me?"

"Certainly!" cried Sung.

And as the ghost was in front, he seized it by the waist. The ghost begged for mercy but Sung killed it, and found the next morning that it was an old fox. That was the end of the trouble in the station-house.

THE DOG FROM THE VILLAGE TAVERN

After Minister Lai Chi-teh of Nanyang died and was buried, he suddenly appeared again, sitting on the sacrificial couch with the same expression, dress and voice as before. He gave instructions to his grandchildren, sons and the women of the house in turn, doing everything in due order, and punished his slaves for their faults. Then, having eaten and drunk, he bade them farewell and went away, leaving his family grief-stricken. For several years he continued to come back from time to time, until the household was disgusted with him. But one day after too much wine he revealed his true form, and they found he was an old dog. When they had beaten it to death, they discovered this was the dog from the village tavern.

THE SERPENT SACRIFICE

In the province of Minchung in Tungyueh, Mount Yungling towers many miles into the air. In its northwest corner there used to live a huge serpent, seventy to eighty feet long and so thick that it took a dozen men to encircle it. The local people went in terror of it, and many officers of Tungyeh, capital of Tungyueh, and other adjoining districts were killed by it. Though they sacrificed oxen and sheep, they had no peace. Then someone dreamed, or some oracle predicted, that this serpent demanded virgins of twelve or thirteen. The authorities were dismayed, but since the serpent continued to make trouble they began supplying it with local girls, especially from the families of criminals. So every eighth month they made a morning sacrifice, setting down the girl at the mouth of the serpent's cave. And the serpent would come out to eat her.

This went on year after year until nine girls had been sacrificed in this way. But when the order came down the tenth time, no virgin could be found. Li Tan of Chianglo County had six daughters but no son, and his youngest daughter Chi offered to go. Her parents would not agree.

"My unhappy parents have six daughters only and no son," said Chi. "So they have no real descendant. We are not like Ti Yung in the Han dynasty who offered to serve as slave in place of her father. Since we cannot work to support our parents, but are simply a burden to them, the sooner we die the better. Besides, my sale will bring in some money for the old folk. Surely this is best!"

Still her parents could not bear to let her go. But in spite of this, Chi left home secretly. Having procured a sharp sword and a dog which could catch snakes, early on the first day of the eighth month she went and sat down in the temple, taking her sword and her dog. As she had put several large rice cakes soaked in honey at the mouth of the cave, very soon the serpent came out. Its head was the size of a bin, its eyes like bronze mirrors two feet in diameter. When it smelt the fragrant cakes and started eating them, Chi loosed her dog to worry it while she cut and wounded it several times from behind. The serpent fled, writhing with pain, but did not get far before it died. Then Chi went into the cave and found the skeletons of the nine other girls. She carried them out and said sadly:

"Because you were timid, the serpent ate you, poor creatures!"

Then she made her way leisurely home.

When the prince of Yueh heard of this he made her his queen, appointed her father magistrate of Chianglo, and richly rewarded her mother and her sisters. Since then there have been no more monsters in Tungyeh, and the local people sing her praises to this day.

DEAD DRUNK

Ti Hsi of Chungshan could brew wine that would make the drinker drunk for a thousand days. Liu Hsuan-shih in his district, who was a heavy drinker, asked Ti for some of this liquor.

"It has just been brewed and not settled yet," Ti told him. "I dare not offer you any."

"Even if the wine is new, won't you give me one cup?" begged Liu.

This Ti did. And Liu asked for more.

"Excellent! Please let me have another cup!"

But Ti said:

"You had better go home now and come back some other time. Just this one cup will make you drunk for a thousand days."

Liu left in some resentment. When he reached home he fell down completely insensible. His family, not suspecting the truth, wept over him and buried him.

Three years later Ti said:

"Liu should have recovered by now from the wine. I must go and see him."

He went to Liu's house and asked:

"Is Hsuan-shih at home?"

The family were amazed.

"He is dead," they said. "The three years' mourning is over."

Ti was shocked and replied:

"Ah, my fine wine sent him to sleep for a thousand days. But now he should be waking."

He bade them dig up the grave and open the coffin. They found hot vapour rising from the grave. Then Ti told them to unseal it, and they saw Liu open his eyes and mouth.

"Wonderful!" he cried. "I have never been so drunk!" And he asked Ti: "What is that brew of yours which has made me so drunk on a single cup that I have only woken up today? What time of day is it now?"

All the men round the grave laughed at him. And those who had sniffed the wine on Liu's breath fell into a drunken stupor for three whole months.

THE OLD WOMAN AND THE SNAKE

In Chiungtu County a poor old woman lived alone. One day while she was having a meal, a small snake with a horn on its head came to her couch, and out of kindness she fed it. This snake grew and grew until it was more than ten feet long, when it killed the local magistrate's best horse. The magistrate was enraged, and demanded that the old woman hand over the snake. She told him that it lived under her bed. The magistrate dug a wide and deep hole, but nothing could he find. Then, in his anger, he had the old woman killed. At that the snake sent a man into a trance and through him demanded of the magistrate:

"Why did you kill my mother? I shall avenge her."

After this there were thunder and wind every night for more than forty days. And when the men of this district met each other, they all asked in surprise:

"How is it that you have the head of a fish?"

One night the whole district, ten miles square with its walled town, sank below the earth and became a lake. It was known as the Sunken Lake. The old woman's house, which was all that was left, is still there to this day. When fishermen go to catch fish they put up there; and if they stay by this house during a storm, all is peaceful and secure. When the wind is calm and the water clear, you can still see the walled town with its towers in the lake. When the water is low, some of the local people go down to fetch wood; for that remains hard, glossy and black. Indeed, pillows made of this timber are often given away as souvenirs.

THE GREAT SERPENT

In Tienmen Principality there are lonely mountains and steep gorges, the gorges high above the plain. Men passing the foot of the mountain often leaped over the forest and disappeared, as if they were fairies with wings. After several such cases had happened in one year, this was called Fairies Valley. Many who wanted to become immortals or were simply curious went there and performed ablutions, hoping they might become fairies. Then they often disappeared.

Finally one man, shrewder than the rest, suspected that some monster was behind this. Accordingly he went deep into the valley, taking a dog with him, and fastened himself to a boulder. When the dog flew off, the man went back and told his fellow-villagers. They gathered several dozen men with sticks to clear the weeds and cut trees until they reached the top of the mountain. There they saw in the distance a great serpent some hundreds of feet long and as high as a man, with ears like winnowing fans. They fell on it and shot it dead. The bones of the men this serpent had devoured were piled high on both sides of it. The serpent's mouth was more than a foot across. It had sucked in all those who had disappeared.

After this the district was safe and free from trouble.

CHIN CHING THE SINGER

Hsueh Tan studied singing under Chin Ching but, unable to master all his art, asked permission to leave. Chin Ching gave him a farewell feast outside the city and, wand in hand, sang a melancholy air. His voice made the forests reverberate and the passing clouds pause to listen. Then Hsueh Tan apologized and begged to be allowed to remain. Never again did he speak of going away.

THE WINE OF IMMORTALITY

An underground passage led from Mount Chun to Pao Mountain in the district of Wu, on the summit of which there were several measures of wine. It was said that those who drank this would become immortal. Emperor Wu Ti of the Han dynasty fasted for seven days and sent several dozen men to fetch this wine from the mountain. He was about to drink it when his jester, Tung-fang Shuo, said:

"I can tell if this is genuine. Let me see it."

With that he drained one cup. When the emperor wanted to kill him, he protested:

"If you kill me, it means the wine is useless. If the wine is really an elixir, how can you kill me?"

Then the emperor pardoned him.

HOW WEI PO-YANG PRETENDED
TO BE DEAD

Wei Po-yang was a native of Wu. Though the son of a noble family, he was interested in Taoist arts. He went into the mountains with three disciples to make an elixir. But after he had succeeded, knowing that his disciples had not yet freed themselves from all thought of worldly pleasure, he determined to test them.

"Though we have the elixir, we should try it out first on the dog," he said. "If the dog flies away, men can take it. If the dog dies, it is unfit for human use."

He gave it to the dog, and the dog died. Then Wei told his disciples:

"Our aim was to obtain an elixir. Now we have it, but the dog has died of it. I fear it is not the will of the gods that we should become immortal, and if we take it we may end like the dog. What shall we do?"

His disciples asked: "Do you mean to try it, master?"

Wei answered: "I have renounced the world and left my family to come to the mountain. If I do not obtain the truth I shall be ashamed to show my face again. So whether I live or die I mean to take it."

But as soon as he put it in his mouth he died. His disciples looked at each other and two of them said:

"We made the elixir in order to become immortals. If eating it kills you, what use is it?"

One disciple, however, said: "Our master is no ordinary man. If he died of the elixir, it must be for some good reason."

So he too took it and died.

The two who were left said to each other: "Our aim in making the elixir was to attain immortality. If eating it kills men, what use is it to us? If we do not take this drug, we shall at least live a few tens of years more."

Therefore instead of taking it, they left the mountain to get coffins for their dead master and the other disciple. After they had gone, Wei Po-yang rose up and put his elixir in the mouth of the dead disciple and the dog. Then they rose up as well. The disciple's name was Yu. They all went off as immortals. On the way they met a woodcutter climbing the mountain, to whom Wei gave a letter of farewell to his friends and neighbours. Then the other two disciples regretted their action.

CHANG TAO-LING AND HIS DISCIPLES

Chang Tao-ling was a native of the principality of Pei, a scholar of the Imperial Academy and well versed in the five classics. But one day he sighed and said:

"This will not serve to prolong life."

He studied the art of achieving immortality, and discovered the way to make the Yellow Emperor's elixir, which must be heated nine times in a cauldron. All the ingredients were costly, and Chang was poor. He therefore became a farmer. But finding he had no talent for managing land and cattle, he gave that up. Then he heard that the men of Shu had integrity and were easy to convert, and that there were holy mountains there. So he went with his disciples to Shu and stayed in Crane Mountain. There he wrote a book on the Way in twenty-four chapters, meditating and strengthening his resolution. One day spirits descended from heaven: thousands of horsemen and equipages with gold carriages and plumed canopies, beside innumerable angels on dragons and tigers. Some called themselves Scribes of the Pillar, others Pages of the Eastern Sea. They taught Chang the Sole Illustrious and Mighty Way, with which he could cure all diseases. Then men flocked to serve him, taking him as their teacher, and tens of thousands of families were converted. He appointed chiefs like local officers to look after these families, and made regulations to govern them. He ordered his disciples to contribute rice, silk and utensils, paper, pens, fuel and other daily necessities. He led them out to make roads, and those who refused to work on the roads fell ill. Bridges and highways needed building, and at his bidding the people did every kind of labour, cutting weeds and clearing cesspools. Those who did not know that this was Chang's work thought these regulations had descended from heaven.

Chang tried to rule with virtue, reluctant to resort to punishment. He drew up rules ordering those who were ill to write down what evil they had done in their lives, then throw the writing into the water and swear to the gods never to commit such crimes again on pain of death. Then all who wanted to avoid disease confessed their sins. This cured them and made them ashamed to repeat their offences, inspiring them with fear of heaven and earth. So sinners mended their ways.

By this means Chang amassed great wealth, with which he bought the drugs to make an elixir. When he had obtained it, he took only half of it, for he did not want to go up to heaven immediately. This enabled him to turn himself into several dozen men. There was a small lake outside his house, and here he often rowed for pleasure while priests and other guests thronged his house, accompanied by another Chang at their feasting while his real self was on the lake.

His method of curing disease was based on general Taoist principles. He changed certain proportions and modified the beginning and the end, but reached the same conclusions. He also used Taoist principles of breath control and diet, instructing his disciples:

"Few of you are free of mundane desires and ready to renounce the world. You can learn my method of breath control and my physical exercises, or how to prolong life through intercourse with women; or you may learn what herbs to take in order to live a few centuries more."

His most important magic principles he taught to Wang Chang only. He predicted, however, that a man from the east would also master them, a man who would arrive on the seventh day of the first month at noon — he described his height and appearance. Sure enough, on that day a man named Chao Sheng, whose looks tallied exactly with the description, did come from the east. Chang gave him seven tests, which he passed successfully. Then Chang initiated him into the secret of the elixir.

He was put to the first of the tests on his arrival, when instead of admitting him they sent men to abuse and humiliate him. He remained in the open for more than forty days, not going away, after which he was admitted.

For his second test he was told to watch the crops and drive wild beasts away. At night a girl of remarkable beauty approached him with the story that she was travelling on a long journey and would like to lodge there. She slept in the next bed, and the following day she said she could not go on because her feet were aching. For several days she stayed there, tempting him, but Chao did not yield to temptation.

The third trial was when Chao found thirty casks of gold by the roadside, but passed by without taking them.

The fourth was when he was sent to gather fuel in the mountain, and three tigers leaped at him and mauled his clothes without injuring him. Chao neither changed colour nor showed fear. Instead he rebuked the tigers: "I am a priest, not guilty of any youthful indiscretions. I have travelled hundreds of *li* to serve my holy master and seek immortality — why should you treat me like this? Have the mountain spirits sent you to test me?" Then the tigers slunk away.

The fifth trial was when Chao bought some dozen rolls of silk in the market and the merchant denied having received the money. Chao gave his own clothes in payment and showed no resentment.

The sixth was when he was watching the crops and a beggar kowtowed to him for alms. Dressed in rags and covered with boils, this fellow was foul and loathsome; but Chao took pity on the man and gave him his own clothes as well as his rations and rice.

The seventh trial took place when Chang led all his disciples to a high cliff among the clouds, above a peach tree as thick as a man's arm which jutted out of the rock over a bottomless abyss. The tree was loaded with fruit, and Chang told his disciples:

"Whichever of you can fetch that fruit will learn the secret of immortality."

His two hundred disciples leaned over to look at the peaches. Their legs trembled and they broke into a cold sweat. They dared not gaze too long. One by one they drew back, protesting that this was not within their power.

Only Chao Sheng said: "If the gods protect me, what danger can there be? Our holy master is here. He will not let me fall to my death. If our master says so, there must be a way to pick these peaches."

He jumped down from the cliff and alighted on the tree without falling. He gathered an armful of peaches. But since the cliff face was steep and had no footholds, he could not climb back again. He therefore tossed the peaches up one by one, two hundred and two in all. Chang gave his disciples one each, ate one himself and left one for Chao. Then he stretched out an arm to help Chao up. The disciples saw their master's arm grow longer and longer till it was over twenty feet and could reach him. Then suddenly Chao was among them, and their master gave him the remaining peach. After Chao had eaten it, their master walked to the edge of the cliff and smiled.

"Because Chao Sheng's heart was pure, he alighted on the tree without falling. I am going to try to do the same, to get some large peaches."

All but Chao Sheng and Wang Chang begged him not to think of it. The master jumped down. Instead of alighting on the tree, however, he vanished completely from sight. Above steep precipices towered all around them, below yawned bottomless chasms, and there was no road. The disciples wept and groaned, but after some time Chao and Wang said to each other:

"If our master has dropped into the bottomless abyss, how can we stay here?"

They both leaped down and landed in front of their master, who was sitting cross-legged on a couch behind a curtain. When he saw them he laughed and said:

"I knew you would come."

He taught them the secret of sainthood. Three days later they went back to their former lodging and found the disciples still fearful and lamenting. Later Chang and these two followers, Chao Sheng and Wang Chang, ascended to heaven in broad daylight. The other disciples gazed after them for a long time till they vanished into the clouds.

When Chang went to the mountain he had taken half the elixir. That was why, though he did not fly up to heaven, he was an immortal on earth. He gave Chao Sheng seven trials to test him, and the result was all he wished.

TSO TZU THE MAGICIAN

Tso Tzu, whose other name was Yuan-fang, was a native of Luchiang well versed in astrology and the five classics. He saw that the Han dynasty was in decline and trouble had broken out all over the empire.

"In days of degeneracy and disorder," he said, "it is dangerous to be a high official and fatal to possess great wealth. It is not worth seeking worldly fame and profit."

He studied philosophy and was so skilled in magic that spirits brought food at his bidding wherever he went. He practised meditation in Tienchu Mountain, and in a stone chamber there found instructions for making the elixir, which enabled him to effect various transformations. The wonders he performed were too many to count.

Lord Tsao Tsao heard of this and sent for him. He shut Tso into a cell and set guards over him, supplying him with no food for a whole year. But Tso came out looking as robust as ever. Tsao Tsao was convinced that he must be a magician, for how else could he dispense with food which is essential to life? He made up his mind to kill him. Tso knew this, however, and begged permission to leave.

"Why do you suddenly want to leave?" asked Tsao Tsao.

"Because you want to kill me," was Tso's reply.

Tsao Tsao denied this, but granted him his wish and prepared a feast for him.

"Since I am going away, let us share a cup of wine," suggested Tso.

65

To this Tsao Tsao agreed. It was winter and the wine, which had been heated, was still too warm to drink. Tso took a pin from his hair to stir the wine, and soon the whole pin disappeared like ink ground on an inkstone. Tsao Tsao had imagined that by sharing the same cup Tso meant he should drink first and then pass the cup on. But Tso simply drew a line in the wine with his pin, and the liquid divided into two separate parts. Tso drank one half and passed the other to Tsao Tsao. And when Tsao Tsao was too suspicious to drink, Tso asked to finish it himself. After draining the wine he threw the cup up to the ceiling, where it hung rocking in the air like a hovering bird. All the guests stared at it, and it did not come down for some time. By then Tso had disappeared, and inquiries revealed that he had gone home.

Then Tsao Tsao was yet more eager to put him to death to see whether he could escape or not. He ordered his arrest. But Tso hid himself among a flock of sheep so that his pursuers could not find him. When they counted the flock and found one more than before, they knew that he had changed into a sheep.

"Our master simply wants to see you," they said. "You had better take your own form again. Don't be afraid."

A large ram came forward and knelt down to ask: "Is that true?"

The officers cried: "There he is!"

They were just about to seize it when all the sheep — several hundred of them — turned into rams and knelt down to ask: "Is that true?"

So once again they did not know which to take.

Later someone came to know of Tso's whereabouts and reported it to Tsao Tsao, who sent to arrest him. This time they captured him, not because he could not escape but because he wished to display his miraculous powers. He was thrown into gaol. When the gaoler came to torture him he found there were two of Tso, one inside the door and one outside, and he could not tell which was true and which was false. When Tsao Tsao heard this he hated Tso even more, and ordered him to be killed in the market-place. But once again they lost him. They closed all the city gates and searched for him. When those who had never seen him asked for his description, the officers said:

"He is blind in one eye and wears a black cloth cap and black clothes. If you see a man like that, arrest him."

Then every living soul in the market-place became blind in one eye and dressed in black, so that Tso could not be found. Tsao Tsao told his men to pursue all these folk and kill any they met. Someone caught such a man and killed him, and reported it to his lord who was well pleased. But when the corpse was brought in for Tsao Tsao's inspection, it was nothing but a bundle of straw — the body had vanished.

Later some men of Chinchow said they had seen Tso Tzu there. And Liu Piao, the governor, determined to seize and execute him for sorcery. Liu Piao drew up his troops, and Tso knew that he hoped to see some magic. Accordingly he strolled over and said to Liu Piao:

"I have a small gift here for each of your soldiers."

Liu Piao said: "You are a stranger and alone. There are many men in my army — how can you make a gift to them all?"

Nevertheless Tso insisted. When Liu Piao sent to see what he had, his men found only one measure of wine and one package of dried meat in a pot. But when they tried to carry these away, not even ten men could lift them. Tso carried these things out himself. He carved the meat and threw it to the ground, asking the help of a hundred men to distribute the wine and meat. Each soldier had three cups of wine and one slice of meat, which tasted like normal meat. When more than ten thousand soldiers had been supplied, there still remained the same amount of wine in the pot, and the meat was not finished either. There were also a thousand guests present at this banquet, all of them got exceedingly drunk. Liu Piao was greatly impressed and dared not kill Tso, who left a few days later and went east to the land of Wu.

He called on a man named Hsu To, who understood magic and lived in Tantu. Some of Hsu's protégés were at the gate with six or seven ox-carts. They lied to Tso: "Hsu To is not at home."

Although he knew this was untrue, Tso left. Then the men's oxen started walking on the tree tops. When they climbed the trees the oxen disappeared, but as soon as they came down the oxen went up again. Brambles one foot long also started growing from their cart-wheels, with thorns which could not be cut, and the wheels would not move when pushed. In consternation they told Hsu:

"An old man came who was blind in one eye. We did not think he was of any consequence, so we lied to him saying you were out. Soon after he left all our ox-carts became bewitched. Can you tell us what this means?"

Hsu said: "Ah, that must have been Tso Tzu who called. How dare you try to fool him? If you hurry you may still catch him."

They went out in different directions in search of him, and when they found him they kowtowed to apologize, and Tso was mollified. He dismissed them, and on their return they found their ox-carts were no longer bewitched.

Then Tso Tzu went to see Sun Tseh, the lord of Wu, who also wanted to kill him. When they went out together, Sun invited Tso to walk in front of his horse, hoping to stab him in the back. Tso Tzu was in wooden sandals. Holding a bamboo cane, he strolled in front. But though Sun Tseh whipped up his horse and pursued him with weapons, he could not overtake him. Realizing that Tso had magic powers, he abandoned the attempt.

Later Tso Tzu told a priest named Keh Hsuan that he meant to go to Huo Mountain to make the elixir. So he left the world of men.

THE PITCHER MAN

No one knows the Pitcher Man's name. More than twenty books of charms for military use, for summoning spirits, for curing diseases and so forth are attributed to him and called *The Pitcher Man's Charms*.

Fei Chang-fang of Junan was an officer in the market. When the Pitcher Man arrived suddenly from a great distance to sell drugs in the market, no one knew him. He set a fixed price for his drugs and could cure all diseases. He would tell his customers:

"After you take this medicine you will vomit such-and-such a thing and be cured on such-and-such a day."

And it came to pass exactly as he said. He made tens of thousands of coins every day, and gave these to the poor and destitute and to those who were hungry and cold, keeping merely thirty to fifty coins for himself. He hung an empty pitcher in his house, and after sunset he would jump into this and disappear. Fei Chang-fang, who saw this from his upper room, was the only one to realize that this stranger was no ordinary mortal. So Fei daily swept the ground before the Pitcher Man's seat and presented him with food and other necessities, none of which was ever declined. This went on for a considerable time, but Fei never wearied, neither did he ask any favours. The Pitcher Man saw that he was to be trusted.

"Come to me this evening when the others have gone," he said.

Fei did as he was told. Then the Pitcher Man said:

"When you see me jump into the pitcher, do the same. You can get into it too."

Fei did so and, sure enough, found himself inside. He saw no pitcher but a fairyland with storeyed buildings, gates and corridors, and dozens of attendants to wait on the Pitcher Man.

"I am an angel," the Pitcher Man told him. "As a punishment for neglecting my work I was sent down from heaven to earth. Because you are an apt pupil you were able to see me."

Then Fei left his seat and bowed.

"I am an ignorant mortal and many are my sins," he said. "Your kindness in taking pity on me is like opening a coffin to give living breath to a corpse, or causing the dead and decayed to rise up and live. I only fear that I am too low and mean to serve you. If you will have compassion on me, I shall be eternally grateful."

"I think very highly of you," replied the other. "But do not speak of this to anyone."

Later the Pitcher Man went to Fei's upper room.

"I have a little wine," he said. "Let us fetch it up and drink together."

Since the wine was downstairs, Fei sent a man for it; but the fellow could not lift the bowl. Several dozen men tried, but none of them could raise it. When Fei told the Pitcher Man this, he went down himself and lifted the bowl with one finger, after which they drank together. The bowl was no larger than a fist, yet they went on drinking till dusk and the wine never failed. Then the Pitcher Man said to Fei:

"I am leaving on such-and-such a day — will you come with me?"

"Words cannot tell how eager I am to accompany you," replied Fei. "But I would like to keep this from my kinsmen. Is that possible?"

"That is easy." The Pitcher Man gave Fei a green bamboo stick. "Take this home and pretend to be ill. Then leave the bamboo on your bed and come away quietly."

71

Fei did as he was told. After he left, his family saw that he had died and his corpse — in fact, the bamboo — was on the bed. They wailed and buried the stick.

Fei accompanied the Pitcher Man as if in a dream. He was left among tigers which ground their teeth and opened their jaws to devour him, but he was not afraid. The next day he was put in a stone cell with a square rock tens of feet across suspended over his head by a straw rope, and many snakes biting the rope so that soon it must be severed. Still Fei remained calm. The Pitcher Man congratulated him.

"You are fit to be taught the truth!"

But when Fei was ordered to eat stinking dung with maggots in it over an inch long, he recoiled. The Pitcher Man sighed and dismissed him, saying:

"You cannot be an angel in heaven, but you can live for hundreds of years on earth." He gave him certain sealed charms, instructing him: "If you keep these you can make spirits do your bidding, cure diseases and avoid calamities." When Fei did not know how to return home, the Pitcher Man gave him a bamboo pole. "Ride on this," he said, "and it will carry you home."

Then Fei rode off on the stick and suddenly, as if awaking from a dream, he found himself home. All his family believed he was a ghost until he explained what had happened and they opened the coffin to find nothing there but a stick. The bamboo pole which he had ridden was thrown into Kepi Pond and turned into a green dragon. Fei fancied he had been away for one day only, but when he asked his family they told him a whole year had passed. Then Fei used his charms to capture ghosts and treat diseases, and there was no one he could not cure. Often, sitting talking with others, he would frown and begin to swear. When questioned he would say:

"I was reproving a ghost."

At that time there was a spirit in Junan which appeared several times a year. It came with outriders and retainers like a governor, entered the local office, sounded drums and made a general tour of inspection before proceeding on its way. This was a great plague. One day Fei went to the yamen just as this spirit was approaching the gate. The governor fled inside, leaving Fei alone. And when the spirit knew who it was it dared not advance.

"Bring that spirit here!" shouted Fei.

The spirit alighted from its carriage and bowed before the court, knocking its head on the ground and swearing to mend its ways.

"Dead, superannuated ghost!" swore Fei. "How dare you bear a grudge and come for no reason with a retinue to make trouble in a government office? You deserve to die for this! Change back to your true form at once!" Then the spirit became a tortoise as big as a cart-wheel, with a head more than ten feet long. Fei ordered it to take a human form, and gave it a sealed charm to deliver to the Lord of Kepi. The ghost bowed and left, weeping, with the charm. Fei sent a man after it, who found the charm standing by the pond and the monster dead with its neck around a tree.

Later Fei went to Tunghai. There had been a great drought for three years, and he told the people who were praying for rain:

"The Lord of Tunghai came here to seduce the Lady of Kepi, and I detained him for trial. But then I forgot to release him. That is why there has been this long drought. Now I shall pardon him and tell him to send down rain."

At once there was a heavy downpour. Fei also had magic means of reducing distance, so that a man could see for hundreds of miles. Then he would extend the distance as before.

TUNG FENG'S MIRACLES

Tung Feng, whose other name was Chun-yi, was a native of Houkuan. During the reign of the first king of Wu, a young magistrate of this district saw that Tung looked about forty and did not realize he was an immortal. But fifty years or more after leaving this post, when he passed through this district again after serving elsewhere, he found all his former subordinates old except Tung Feng, who seemed completely unchanged.

"Are you a saint?" he asked Tung. "This is how you looked fifty years ago. Now I am a hoary old man, but you seem younger than ever. How is this?"

"A mere matter of chance," said Tung.

Tu Hsieh, the prefect of Chiaochow, was poisoned and died. Three days after his death Tung Feng happened to pass that way. He put three pills in the dead man's mouth, poured water down his throat, and gave orders for his head to be raised and the pills shaken down. Then the corpse's limbs began to move, colour came to his cheeks and in half a day he set up. Four days later he was able to speak, and he told them that his death had been like a dream. A dozen men in black took him to a carriage. He passed through a great red gate and was thrown into prison. There were separate cells, each holding one prisoner only, and Tu was put in one of these cells which was sealed up with earth so that no light could enter. Then he heard a voice outside announce that Tai Yi, the chief of the gods, had sent for him and the earth outside his cell should be removed. After some time he was led out to a carriage with a red canopy in which three men were sitting. One of these, holding a tally, told him to mount. But before he reached his own house he woke and was restored to life. He rose to thank Tung, saying:

"I am so much in your debt that how can I ever repay you?"

He built a storeyed building for him in the court. Tung would take no food except dried dates and wine, and three times every day the prefect supplied him with these. Each time Tung came for food and drink he passed through the air like a bird, and flew off after he had finished without being observed. After more than a year like this he decided to leave. Shedding tears, Tu tried to keep him, but to no purpose.

"Where are you going?" he asked. "Do you want a large boat?"

"I need no boat but a coffin."

So Tu made ready a coffin. The next day at noon Tung died without any warning, and Tu put him in the coffin and buried him. Seven days later, a man from Yungchang brought the prefect Tung's respects. Then Tu opened the coffin and found nothing in it but a piece of silk, with a human figure painted on one side and a charm in vermilion on the other.

Later Tung went to live at the foot of Lu Mountain in the prefecture of Yuchang. A man there who was nearly dying of leprosy was carried to him, and kowtowed to beg for his help. Tung told them to put him in a room, cover him with five layers of cloth, and not allow him to move. The leper said that first some creature came to lick him, and this was agony. It licked all over him from head to foot with a tongue which must have been over a foot wide. It breathed hard like an ox, but he could not tell what manner of thing it was. After it had gone Tung took him to the pool and bathed him, then sent him away with a warning:

"You will soon be well, but take care not to catch cold."

For about a dozen days the man was as red as if he had been flayed, and suffered torment. But the pain was relieved by washing. After twenty days he recovered and grew a new skin — one that was white and smooth.

One year there was a great drought, and Magistrate Ting Shih-yen said to his men: "I hear Tung Feng has magic power. He must be able to bring rain."

He went in person with food and wine to see Tung and told him about the drought.

"It is easy to get rain," said Tung. But then he looked at his house. "My poor home is open to the elements. What shall I do if it rains?"

The magistrate took the hint.

"If you can get us rain, we shall lose no time in building you a good house."

The next day a hundred officers and men, headed by the magistrate, carried bamboo and wood there to erect a house. To mix the plaster with mud, they would have to fetch water from several miles away.

"There is no need," said Tung. "It will pour with rain this evening."

So they did not go. And that night torrential rain flooded the place, causing general rejoicing.

Tung Feng lived in the mountains and did not work in the fields. He treated the sick every day and took no payment. But when he cured a man of a serious illness, he asked him to plant five apricot trees, and those who had not been so ill he asked to plant one. In this way, in a few years' time, he had a fine orchard of more than a hundred thousand trees, where he let the birds and beasts of the mountain frolic. But the grass there never grew rank — it always seemed newly mown. When Tung had a rich crop of apricots, he built a thatched barn in the forest and announced:

"Any man who wants apricots need not pay me. Just leave one measure of grain in the barn and take away one measure of apricots."

If men took away more apricots than they brought grain, tigers came out of the forest to chase them, roaring. They fled in terror and some of the apricots would fall by the wayside, so that when they reached home and weighed the fruit it equalled their grain exactly. If a man stole apricots, tigers would pursue him all the way home and kill him. But when his family sent the fruit back and apologized to Tung for his dishonesty, the dead man would revive. So every year Tung exchanged his apricots for grain with which he relieved the poor and destitute, as well as wayfaring men. Each year he gave away more than twenty thousand bushels.

The local magistrate's daughter was incurably bewitched by some evil spirit. The magistrate came to Tung and said:

"If you will cure my daughter, I shall send her to serve you."

Tung agreed and summoned the spirit — a white crocodile tens of feet long. The crocodile crawled to the sick girl's door, and Tung bade the servants kill it. Then the girl was cured and Tung made her his wife, but they never had any children. As Tung was often away from home and his wife was lonely, she adopted a girl in her teens. One day Tung soared up to heaven and disappeared in the clouds. His widow and daughter stayed on in the house, supporting themselves by selling apricots. If anyone tried to cheat them, tigers rushed out after him. Tung lived for more than three hundred years on earth, but never looked much older than thirty.

CHI KANG AND THE HEADLESS GHOST

Chi Kang was a man of noble character who liked to roam the country. Travelling south-west of Loyang, he once came to a station named Huayang a few dozen *li* from the capital, where he put up for the night. There was no one else there that day: he was all alone. The station stood on an old execution ground, and accidents often happened to those who lodged there; but Chi Kang, who had a clear conscience, was not afraid. At about the first watch he started strumming his lyre, and ran through several tunes. He was an excellent performer, and a voice from the void called:

"Bravo!"

Chi Kang stopped playing.

"Who are you?"

"I am a dead man. I have been here for thousands of years. When I heard such a sweet and harmonious performance on the lyre I could not help coming to listen, for I used to love music too. Unfortunately I was killed unjustly and my body mutilated, which makes me unfit to be seen. But I greatly admire your playing and would like to watch you if you have no objection. Do go on."

After making some more music, Chi Kang struck his lyre and cried:

"It is growing late. Won't you show yourself? Why should we stand on ceremony?"

Then the ghost appeared, holding its head in its hand.

"After hearing you play my heart feels light," it said. "I seem to have come to life again."

So they discussed their common interest in music, and the spectre's comments were lucid and impassioned. Finally it asked Chi Kang: "May I borrow your lyre?"

Chi Kang invited it to play. Some of the tunes it strummed were common enough, but one piece called *Kuang Ling San* was quite superb. Chi Kang learned this from the ghost, memorizing the whole of it within a few hours, for this was a better melody than ever he had heard before. The ghost made him swear not to teach it to others and not to disclose the ghost's name. Just before dawn it said:

"Although we met only this night, we have formed a thousand years' friendship. Now the long night is over. Much against my will I must leave you!"

THE MISCHIEVOUS GHOSTS

During the Tsin dynasty there lived on the east mount of Wuchangpu of Wuchang a man named Chou Tzu-chang. In the third year of Hsien-kang (337) he called on the Chi family in Hanhsipu, a few *li* from his home. On his way back, some hundred yards from his house, he saw the empty mount in front suddenly fill with tiled houses, and guards seized him by the neck.

"I am a disciple of Buddha!" protested Chou. "How can you arrest me?"

"You say you are Buddha's disciple," mocked the ghosts. "Can you chant sutras?"

Chou knew *The Four Heavenly Kings* and *The Young Stag*. He chanted these several times, but still the ghosts would not release him. Knowing that they were ghosts, he swore at them.

"You crack-brained spectres, you! Haven't I told you that I'm Buddha's disciple and chanted all those verses for you? Why don't you let me go?"

Then they loosed him and the houses in front disappeared, but they went on dogging his steps. When he came to his gate they barred the way and would not let him in. Chou said nothing but decided to take them to the Hanhsi Monastery. Accordingly he seized one by the chest.

"You ghostly imbecile! We'll settle this before the monks."

The ghost clutched hold of Chou too, and they dragged each other westward. Then the ghosts behind shouted:

"Let him go! He wants to take you west to the monastery."

So the other ghost set him free. Chou taunted his pursuers:

"There are priests in the monastery — aren't you afraid?"

But one ghost behind him whispered:

"Take a look at that priest in the east city. How did he get that scratch on his face?"

They shrieked with ghostly laughter.

It was after midnight when Chou finally reached home.

THE TWO HUNTERS

One day Yuan Hsiang and Ken Shuo of Yenhsien in the principality of Kuaichi went out hunting. After crossing many hills and ridges, they sighted six or seven wild goats and gave chase. The goats crossed a steep, narrow stone bridge, and the hunters followed. Then they scaled a sheer red precipice named Red Wall Mountain. Water cascaded down it like white cloth, and a cave seemed to serve as an entrance. Going in, they found a great plain inside where all the herbs and trees were aromatic. In a hut they discovered two girls of about sixteen, girls of most remarkable beauty, dressed in blue. One was named Glistening Pearl, the other. . . . These girls seemed overjoyed to see the hunters.

"We have looked forward so long to your coming!" they cried.

So the men took them as their wives.

One day the two girls went out.

"A friend of ours has found a husband," they said. "We must go to congratulate her."

Their sandals tinkled as they crossed the precipice; and the two hunters, who were homesick, stole away. But the girls caught them as they were making off. They agreed to let the men go, and gave them a pouch which they told them never to open. Then the hunters returned to their homes.

One day some time after, when they were out, one of their household opened the pouch. It was made like a lotus with layer upon layer of pearls, and as soon as they reached the fifth layer a small blue bird flew out. The men learned of this on their return, but by then it was too late for anything but regret. The next day they went ploughing and their families sent them the noonday meal as usual, but found them lying motionless in the fields. When their relatives went up to look, they were nothing but husks like the skins sloughed by cicadas.

THE LADY OF THE WHITE STREAM

During the reign of Emperor An[1] of Tsin there lived a young man in the county of Hokuan named Hsieh Tuan. Left an orphan early without any kinsmen, he was brought up by a neighbour. And by the age of eighteen he was a modest, respectable and law-abiding fellow. He began to keep house for himself, but as he was not yet married all his neighbours were concerned for him and wanted to find him a wife. So far, however, none of them had succeeded.

Each day Hsieh rose up early and sat up late, working hard in the fields from dawn till dusk. One day near his hamlet he found an enormous snail as big as a three-pint pot, and took it home as a curiosity to keep it in a jar for a couple of weeks. After that, whenever he went in from the fields he found hot food and drink and the fire ready lit. Thinking his kind neighbour must have done this for him, a few days later he went over to thank him.

"None of my doing," said his neighbour. "You have no call to thank me."

Hsieh thought the good man must have misunderstood him. When the same thing had happened repeatedly he questioned him again. His neighbour laughed.

"I know you have taken a wife on the sly, and she is cooking for you. Why say it is my doing?"

Hsieh was dumbfounded, completely at a loss. One day he left home at cockcrow but stole back during the morning to peep through the fence. He saw a young girl come out of the jar and start lighting the fire in the

---

[1]A.D. 397-418.

kitchen. Going in to look for the snail, he realized it had changed into the girl. He walked into the kitchen.

"Where did you come from, young lady?" he asked. "And why are you cooking for me?"

The girl was most put out and tried in vain to take refuge in the jar.

"I am the Lady of the White Stream in the Milky Way," she told him. "Because you lived such a virtuous life, the Heavenly Emperor took pity on your loneliness and sent me to keep house for you for a time. In less than ten years you will become rich and find a wife, and then I should have left you. But now that you have surprised me for no reason, discovering my true form, I cannot stay. I must leave you. However, you will do better from now on if you work hard on the land and make extra money by fishing and cutting wood. I shall give you this shell as well. Use it as a grain container. You will never find it empty."

He entreated her to stay but she refused. A sudden storm blew up and off she flew.

Then Hsieh set up a shrine and sacrificed to this goddess at festivals. And though not very rich he always had enough to live on. Later his neighbours found him a wife, and he became a magistrate. The Temple of the Lady of the White Stream stands to this day at the roadside.

THE FAITHFUL DOG

During the Tai Ho period (366-371) of the Tsin dynasty, a man named Yang of Kuangling had a dog to which he was very much attached. He took it wherever he went. Once he fell into a drunken sleep in the marshland just when men came to burn the reeds, for it was winter and there was a strong wind. The dog took fright and howled, but Yang was too drunk to realize his danger. Since there was a pool in front, the dog plunged into it, coming back to sprinkle water on the grass all around. It did this several times, describing a circle, until all the grass around was wet. Thus when the fire reached them they were not burned. Yang knew nothing of this till he woke.

On another occasion, walking in the dark, Yang fell into an empty well. His dog howled till morning when a man passed by and was surprised to find a dog howling there. Upon looking into the well he discovered Yang.

"If you get me out, sir," said Yang, "I promise to repay you well."

"Give me this dog and I will."

"This dog has saved my life. I can't give it away. Ask me for anything else."

"In that case, stay where you are."

Then the dog looked down into the well and Yang understood its meaning.

"Very well," he told the passer-by. "You shall have the dog."

At that the fellow helped him out, tied a rope round the dog's neck and led it away.

Five days later the dog came back to Yang by night.

THE HUNTER

During the second half of the third century, a man of Linhai went to the hills to hunt. He lodged in the forest. One night there came to him a man ten feet tall in a yellow gown and white belt.

"Tomorrow I fight my enemy," said this man. "If you will help me, I shall reward you well."

"I will help if I can," said the hunter. "Why speak of reward?"

"Go to the stream tomorrow, at the hour for the noonday meal. My foe will come from the north, I from the south. My belt will be white, his yellow."

The hunter agreed.

The next morning when he went out he heard sound like a storm north of the stream and found all the trees and undergrowth trampled down. It was the same on the south side. Then he saw two huge snakes over one hundred feet long at the stream, coiling about each other. As the white snake was being worsted, the hunter raised his crossbow and shot the yellow snake dead.

At dusk the same man came to thank him, saying:

"You may stay here and hunt for a year. But leave next year and on no account return. Otherwise on your own head be it."

"Very good," said the hunter.

So he stayed there for one year, and bagged so much game that he became very rich.

A few years later, remembering how well he had done in that region but forgetting the warning given him, he went back. Then the man in the white belt told him:

"I warned you not to return, but you would not listen. Now my enemy's sons have grown and will certainly avenge themselves on you. I am powerless to help you."

When the hunter heard this he was greatly dismayed and turned to flee. But three men eight feet high all in black appeared. They approached with gaping jaws, and the hunter fell dead.

THE KING OF THE ANTS

Tung Chao-chih of Tangyang County was being ferried across the Chientang River when in midstream he saw an ant scurrying to and fro on a short reed, gazing round in evident panic.

"So even insects fear death!" he exclaimed

He tied a string to the reed to enable the ant to crawl up to the prow. But the boatman swore:

"Don't save that ant — it has a poisonous sting. If you do, I shall stamp on it."

Tung had pity on the creature, however. When the boat reached the shore the ant escaped by crawling up the string.

In the middle of the night Tung dreamed that a man in black came in, followed by a hundred others. This stranger thanked him, saying:

"I am the king of the ants. I was careless enough to fall into the river and you, sir, saved my life. If you are ever in difficulties be sure to let me know!"

More than ten years later revolts and risings broke out on every side south of the river. Tung was passing the Yuhang Mountains when he was thrown into Yuhang gaol on the charge of being a brigand leader. He suddenly remembered his dream about the king of the ants. His fellow prisoners asked him what he was thinking.

"The king of ants said I should call him if ever I was in difficulties," he told them. "But how can I send him a message?"

One of the prisoners said: "Just hold a few ants in your palm and pray to them."

Tung did this. And that night he dreamed that the man in black appeared and said:

"Go at once to the Yuhang Mountains. The emperor will soon issue a general amnesty."

Tung awoke to find that the ants had bitten through his wooden pillory, enabling him to escape. He crossed the river and fled into the mountains. Then the amnesty was issued and he was spared.

MAN INTO TIGER

In the year 376, Hsieh Tao-hsun of Anlu County in the principality of Chianghsia was twenty-two. Hsieh had passed a normal childhood, but now he contracted a disease which sent him out of his mind. Nothing could cure him. He took drugs and ran completely wild. Then he suddenly vanished and turned into a tiger, and there was no counting the number of people he ate. One of his victims was a woman who was plucking mulberry leaves. After devouring her he hid her trinkets in the rocks where he could come back for them when he turned into a man again.

After a year of this, he resumed his human form and returned home. Later he became an official, serving as a secretary at court. One night while chatting with others about strange happenings in heaven and earth, he admitted that he had once fallen ill, lost his reason, and changed into a tiger to prey on human beings for a year — he gave the names and localities of some of his victims. Among those present were men whose fathers, sons or brothers he had eaten. How bitterly they wailed! They seized him and haled him before the authorities, and finally he starved to death in Chienkang gaol.

THE WILD-CATS

On Kuopu Mountain there stood a shrine with a station-house beside it. There Lu Ssu put up one night with his young wife — and there he lost her. Going in search of her, he found a walled town with an office in which an official in a gauze cap was sitting at the desk. This official's followers fell on Lu, who cut and thrust with his sword till he had killed more than a hundred of them. At that the rest scattered, while the dead turned into dead wild-cats. Looking at the office he found it was a huge ancient tomb, open on top so that one could see inside clearly. There were women in the tomb, among them his wife who seemed to have fainted away. He carried her out and went back to fetch the others, several dozen in all. On some of their bodies the hair was beginning to grow. Some had hair on their feet and faces, having turned into cats. At dawn Lu took his wife back to the station-house, and explained to the station-master what had happened. Several dozen families had lost a daughter there. The local officer escorted them to the tomb to recover these women, and announced the news to families far and near so that each might send for its lost wife or daughter. The following year there were no further manifestations at the shrine.

THE HOUND AS GO BETWEEN

During the Han dynasty, Huang Yuan of the principality of Taishan opened his gate one morning to find a black hound sitting outside keeping watch, as if it belonged to the house. Huang fastened it to a lead and took it out on a hunt with some neighbouring lads. When dusk was falling he saw a deer and loosed the hound, which ran so fast that try as he might he could not catch up with it. After following it for several *li* he reached a mountain cave. He went in for about a hundred yards till he came to a highway flanked with ash and willow trees, with walls on either side. Then Huang followed the hound through a gate. He found several dozen rooms within, filled with beautiful girls in splendid attire, engaged in strumming lyres, plucking harps or playing draughts.

When he reached the north pavilion, he found three rooms with two maids in attendance. At the sight of Huang, they looked at each other and smiled.

"This is the husband the hound has brought for Miaoyin!"

One maid stayed there while the other went inside. Soon four maids came out and announced that Madame Tai-chen had this proposal for Huang:

"I have a daughter who is now fifteen and old enough to marry. Fate has destined her to be your wife."

When night fell Huang was led into a hall with a southern exposure which overlooked a lake. There was a pavilion in the lake, with entrances at the four corners. It was brightly lit and had curtains and a couch inside. Miao-yin was a ravishing beauty, and her maids were pretty girls too. After the wedding was over, they feasted and went to bed. A few days later Huang wanted to go home to announce his marriage to his family.

"Mortals differ from immortals," sighed Miao-yin. "We cannot be together for long after all."

The next day she gave him her jade pendant as a parting gift, and shed tears by the steps.

"We cannot remain together although I love you so dearly! Think of me on the first of each third month, and fast and purify yourself on that day."

The four maids saw Huang out, and in half a day he reached home. He longed for his fairy wife, and each year at the appointed time he would catch a glimpse of her carriage gliding through the air.

THE WAKE

An old man in Kuchang County lived with his daughter in the mountains. In the year 361, Kuang of Yuhang asked for the girl's hand in marriage, but her father refused him. Later the old man died of illness, and his daughter set off to the city to buy a coffin. On the way she met Kuang and told him what had happened.

"I am in desperate trouble," she confided. "If you will go home to watch by my father's corpse till I come back, I promise to marry you." When Kuang agreed she told him: "You will find a pig in the pigsty. Kill it and eat it."

When Kuang reached their house he heard clapping and dancing and sounds of merriment inside. He dashed in and found a crowd of ghosts in the hall, holding the corpse and having sport with it. Brandishing his cane and shouting at the top of his voice, he charged at them and put the ghosts to flight. Then he watched beside the corpse and slaughtered the pig. That night an old ghost appeared beside the corpse and stretched out its hand for some flesh. Kuang seized its arm and held it so tight that it could not get away. Outside the door he heard the other ghosts hooting:

"Serve the old fool right for his greed!"

"It was you who killed the old man," said Kuang accusingly. "Hurry up and bring back his spirit, and I'll let you go. Otherwise I shall never free you."

The old ghost said: "It was really my children who killed him."

He called to them to bring the spirit back. Then by degrees the old man returned to life, and Kuang let the old ghost go. When the girl came back with the coffin, she was overcome with grief and joy at this sight. And so Kuang married her.

THE BIRD THAT COULD SPEAK

When Minister Huan Huo of the Tsin dynasty was governor of Chingchow, he had a lieutenant who trimmed a mynah's tongue on the fifth day of the fifth month, and taught the bird to speak. That mynah could talk about anything under the sun, and join in conversations. The lieutenant was a good performer on the lute, and the bird often stayed by him to listen to the music. It could imitate men's laughter and voices too. When the minister met with his officers, he would ask the bird to mimic the guests' voices, and this it did very well. One man had a muffled voice which was difficult to reproduce. The bird attempted and failed; but as soon as it put its head into a pitcher, the imitation sounded perfect.

One day a steward stole something in front of the bird. When the lieutenant went to the privy and the mynah saw there was no one else in sight, it secretly informed against the steward. The lieutenant bore this in mind, but said nothing at the time. Then the steward stole some beef, and once more the mynah reported this to its master.

"You say he has taken some beef," said the lieutenant. "But where is the evidence?"

"In a fresh lotus leaf behind the screen," said the mynah. And there, indeed, it was.

The lieutenant punished the steward very severely, and in his rage the man scalded the bird to death. The lieutenant grieved for days, and wanted the steward killed to avenge his mynah.

The minister said: "In view of your grief over the loss of your pet, I feel the man deserves death. But we cannot kill a man because of a bird."

So the steward was sentenced to five years' penal servitude.

WOMAN INTO CAT

In the year 371 a man's mother died and he was too poor to give her a fitting funeral. He therefore took the coffin to the mountain and started building a tomb himself, working day and night beside the dead. When dusk fell, a woman came with a child in her arms to rest there. The filial son worked through the night, but the woman curled up to sleep beside the fire. And while she slept her true form was revealed — she was a wild cat with a black chicken between her paws! He killed her and threw the body into a pit behind. The next day a man came up to him:

"Where is my wife? She broke her journey here last night."

"There was only a wild cat, and that I killed."

"You have murdered my wife! How dare you call her a cat? Where is she now?"

When they went to the pit to look, the cat had changed back again into a dead woman. The man tied him up and took him to court, demanding that he pay with his life.

Then the son said to the magistrate: "I swear this fellow is a monster. Bring out a hound, and you will see for yourself."

The magistrate asked the man whether he understood hunting and could judge a hound for him.

"I am afraid of dogs," was the hasty reply. "I cannot tell you anything about them."

The instant the magistrate let out a hound, the man changed into an old wild cat. When they had shot it they looked at the dead woman again, and she had also changed back into a cat.

THE POWDER GIRL

A very rich couple had an only son, to whom they were devoted. At the market one day he saw a beautiful girl selling powder made of white lead, and fell in love with her. But with no one to introduce him he had to make buying powder his pretext to go there. He went to her stall every day, and left without a word after making his purchase. As time went by the girl became suspicious. The next day when he came she asked him:

"What do you do with all that powder?"

He told her that he loved her but had not dared introduce himself, using this as a pretext to see her. The girl was touched and agreed to meet him the following evening.

That night the young man lay waiting in his room for her. At dusk, sure enough, she came. He was in raptures. Embracing her, he said:

"Now my wish is granted!"

In an excess of joy he died.

The girl was terrified. At her wit's end, she ran back to the powder shop. When it was time for breakfast, the lad's parents were surprised that he did not appear, and going to look, found him dead.

Before burying him they opened his cases and stacked there they discovered over a hundred packets of powder, large and small.

"This powder must have killed my son!" declared his mother.

She went to the market to all the powder-vendors, and at the girl's stall found the same packaging. She laid hold of her and demanded:

"Why did you kill my son?"

At this the girl burst out crying and told the truth. The young man's parents did not believe her though, and haled her to the court on a murder charge.

"I am not afraid to die," she said. "But let me see him once more and mourn over him."

The magistrate agreed.

She clasped the lad's body and wept bitterly.

"Alas that we should end like this!" she sighed. "But if our spirit lives after death, I shall die content."

All of a sudden the young man came back to life, and recounted all that had happened. He and the girl became husband and wife, and were blessed with many descendants.

THE MAGISTRATE AND THE
LOCAL DEITY

Chen Chung, a native of Chungshan, was appointed magistrate of Yuntu. On his way to his post he was informed that the son of the local deity wished to call on him. Soon a young, handsome god arrived and they exchanged the usual courtesies.

"I am here at my father's behest," announced the young god. "He longs to be allied to your noble house, and hopes you will take my younger sister in marriage. I have come to bring you this message."

"I am past my prime and have one wife already." Chen was taken aback. "How can I do such a thing?"

"My sister is young and remarkably beautiful. We must find a good match for her. How can you refuse?"

"I am old and have a wife. It would not be right."

They argued back and forth several times, but Chen remained adamant. The young god looked put out.

"Then my father will come himself," he said. "I doubt if you can refuse him."

He left, followed on both banks of the river by a large retinue of attendants with caps and whips.

Soon the local deity arrived in person with an equipage like a baron's. His carriage had a dark-green canopy and red reins and was escorted by several chariots. His daughter rode in an open carriage with several dozen silk pennants and eight maids before it, all of them dressed in embroidered gowns more splendid than mortal eye has ever seen. They pitched a tent on the bank near Chen and spread a carpet. Then the deity alighted and sat by a low table on a white woollen rug. He had a jade spittoon, a hat-box of tortoise-shell and a white fly-whisk. His daughter remained on the east bank, with eunuchs carrying whisks at her side and maids in front. The local deity ordered his assistant officers, some sixty of them, to sit down before him, and called for music. The instruments they used seemed to be of glass.

"I have a humble daughter dear to my heart," said the deity. "Since you come of a renowned and virtuous family, we are eager to be connected with you by marriage. That is why I sent my son with this request."

"I am old and my health is failing," replied Chen Chung. "I already have a wife and my son is quite big. Much as I am tempted by this proffered honour, I must beg to decline."

"My daughter is twenty," continued the deity. "She is beautiful and gentle, and possesses all the virtues. As she is now on the bank, there is no need for any preparations. The wedding can take place at once."

Still Chen Chung stood out stubbornly, and even called the deity an evil spirit. He drew his sword and laid it on his knees, determined to resist to the death, and refused to discuss the matter any further. The local deity flew into a passion. He summoned three leopards and two tigers, which opened wide their crimson mouths and shook the earth with their roars as they leaped at Chen. They attacked several dozen times, but Chen held them at bay till dawn when the deity withdrew, thwarted. He left behind one carriage and several dozen men to wait for Chen, however. Then Chen moved into the Huihuai County office. The waiting carriage and men followed him in, and a man in plain clothes and cap bowed to him and advised him to stay there and not go any further.

Chen Chung did not dare leave for another ten days. Even then he was followed home by a man in a cap with a whip. And he had not been back many days before his wife contracted an illness and died.

THE WOUNDED GHOST

In their youth Liu Tao-hsi and his younger cousin, Kang-tsu, did not believe in ghosts. Their elder cousin, Hsin-po, who could see supernatural beings, was quite unable to convince them. One day, east of a house near Changkuang Bridge at Chingko, Hsin-po told them there was a murderous ghost on the east fence. Tao-hsi laughed and asked the place. Then pulling Hsin-po with him, he drew his long sword to kill the spectre. Hsin-po behind him shouted:

"The ghost is going to hit you!"

Before Tao-hsi reached the fence there came a great thwack like the sound made by the larger bastinado, and Tao-hsi fell to the ground. He did not come to himself till the next day, and it took him a month to recover.

Then Hsin-po told them:

"There is a ghost on the mulberry tree east of the office. It is still small now. Once it grows up it will make trouble."

Kang-tsu did not believe this and asked to be shown the exact place on the tree. About ten days later there was a dark, moonless night and Tao-hsi, under cover of the darkness, struck the place where the ghost was with his halberd and left again unknown to all. The next day Hsin-po passed by early and gave a shout.

"Who struck this ghost last night?" he cried in amazement. "It cannot move. Very soon it will be dead."

At that Kang-tsu roared with laughter.

THE LOVELORN SPIRIT

Pang O of the principality of Chulu was a strikingly handsome man. A daughter of the Shih family in that district fell in love with him at first sight, and when later she was seen calling on him his wife grew extremely jealous. One day hearing the girl coming, she bade her maids tie her up and take her home; but on the way the young lady vanished like smoke. When the maids reported this to her family, the girl's father was astounded.

"My daughter has not left the house," he said. "How dare you slander us?"

Pang's father watched his son carefully, however, and discovered the girl in the young man's study one night. He seized her and took her home. When her own father saw her, he was completely amazed.

"I have just left the inner chambers," he explained, "I saw my daughter there working with her mother. How can she be in two places?"

He told servants to summon his daughter, and the moment the real girl appeared the other vanished. The puzzled father told his wife to investigate, and the girl explained that after peeping at Pang O once when he was in their hall she had dreamed ever since of going to his home, and had been caught by his wife when she went in.

"Well, I never!" exclaimed her father. "Evidently when a spirit is deeply moved, it can assume any form it chooses. So what vanished was your spirit after all."

The girl resolved not to marry anyone else. A year later, however, Pang's wife contracted some strange disease which proved incurable. Then Pang sent betrothal gifts to the Shih family and married their daughter.

THE CEDAR PILLOW

The priest of Chiaohu Temple had a pillow made of cedar. After a good thirty years in his possession a small crack appeared in its back. Tang Lin of this county, while travelling on business, happened to enter this temple to pray for good fortune. The priest asked if he was married, and told him to creep into the crack in the pillow. He did so, and found vermilion gates, marble palaces and towers, more magnificent than any to be seen on earth. There he met Marshal Chao who found him a wife, by whom he had six children, four boys and two girls. After that he was recommended for the post of imperial librarian and then promoted to the rank of imperial secretary. So he lived in the pillow with no thought of his home, until at last things went ill for him. Then the priest called him out, and he emerged. Though many years had passed within the pillow, a short time only had elapsed outside.

THE NEW GHOST

A new ghost, wasted and haggard, met an old friend who had been dead for about twenty years and now looked fat and sleek.

"How are you?" asked his friend, when they had greeted each other.

"I am so hungry I can hardly stand it. You must know all the dodges. Tell me what to do."

"That is easy. Frighten men by working wonders, and they will give you food."

The new ghost went to the east side of the village, where he found a family of devoted Buddhists. There was a mill to the west of the house, and the ghost started turning the mill as he had in life. The master of the house said to his children:

"Buddha has taken pity on our poverty and sent this ghost to turn the mill for us."

He brought up cartloads of wheat, until by night the ghost had ground dozens of bushels and had to leave exhausted.

"You cheated me!" he swore at his friend.

"Try again. Next time you'll get food."

So he went to the west side of the village to a family of devoted Taoists. There was a mortar by the gate, and the ghost started pounding the pestle as he had in life.

"Yesterday this ghost helped someone else," said the master of the house. "Today it has come to help me. Let us carry grain to it."

He bade the maids winnow grain, and by evening the ghost was worn out, but not a bite or sup had he received. He went back that night in a passion.

"We are relatives by marriage, not ordinary friends!" he accused the other ghost. "Why should you cheat me? I have slaved for two whole days but not got one bowl of food."

"You have simply been unlucky," replied his friend. "It is hard to make any impression on Buddhists and Taoists. If you work wonders in ordinary households, you are bound to be given food."

Then the new ghost went to a house with a bamboo pole at its gate. Going in, he saw women eating by one window. There was a white dog in the courtyard, and the ghost picked this up so that it seemed to be walking on air. When the family saw this they were amazed, and declared they had never seen such a wonder before. They consulted a fortune-teller.

"You have a hungry visitor," he told them. "All will be well if you kill the dog and sacrifice it in the courtyard with sweetmeats, wine and rice."

They did this, and the ghost made a hearty meal. After that he took his friend's advice and went on working wonders.

HEART'S DESIRE

There was once a young man named Ou Ming of Lu-
ling, who often accompanied merchants on their trips.
Whenever he crossed Lake Pengcheh he tossed valuables
off the boat as a gift for the god of the lake. Some
years later when making this crossing, a broad, dusty
highway opened before him in the water and officers rode
up to him in carriages or on horseback, announcing that
they came from Lord Ching Hung. He knew that these
were not mortals, but dared not refuse to go with them.
Then he saw in the distance a government office with
functionaries and guards at the gate, and was afraid he
would not return alive. But the officers reassured him:

"You have nothing to fear! You have given so many
gifts to Lord Ching Hung that he wants to entertain
you. He will certainly make you rich presents. But
do not accept them — ask for Heart's Desire."

Sure enough, when Ou Ming reached the place the
lord offered him silk and other gifts. But he refused
these and asked for Heart's Desire. The deity was
amazed, and Ou could see that he was loath to consent.
Against his will, however, he called for Heart's Desire
and ordered her to go with Ou Ming. Heart's Desire
was one of the lord's maids, from whom he could get
whatever he set his heart on.

When Ou took Heart's Desire back with him, all his
wishes were granted and within a few years he was very
rich. Then he grew proud and ceased to love her. One
New Year's Day at cockcrow he called for her, but Heart's
Desire did not come at once. He flew into a rage then
and wanted to beat her, whereupon she took to her heels.

He chased her to the rubbish heap, which was covered

with a pile of brushwood swept up on New Year's Eve, and with that she made good her escape. Ou did not know this, however, but thought she was hiding in the rubbish heap. He beat it with his stick to drive her out. After a long time, when she failed to emerge, he knew that he could not force her.

"If you will make me rich, I promise not to beat you again!" he cried.

That is why men beat the rubbish heap on New Year's Day at cockcrow — they believe this will bring them wealth.

THE DEAD MAN'S SON

When Hsieh Miao-chih was governor of Wuhsin, one of his attendants, Tsou Lan, was following the troops with a boat of firewood. He reached Pingwang Station one rainy evening when the troops in front had halted for the night. The boat was open and afforded no shelter; but across the bay Tsou saw a lighted window, and towards this he made his way. He found a thatched hut. There a man of fifty or thereabouts was making mats, while on the bed lay a boy of ten. Tsou asked them to put him up for the night, and the man agreed willingly. The child was sobbing bitterly, and though the man tried to console him he went on sobbing till dawn. Tsou inquired the reason.

"This is my son," the man told him. "Now his mother wants to marry again, and he is crying because he misses her."

Just before dawn Tsou left. But when he looked back he could see no hut, only two graves overgrown with weeds and brambles. As he was leaving, he met a woman in a boat.

"Where do you come from?" she asked. "Not a soul lives here."

Tsou told her his adventure.

"That was my son!" she said. "I was going to marry again, and am on my way to say goodbye to them."

With tears in her eyes she went to the graves and burst out weeping. Then she gave up her second marriage.

THE SCHOLAR BY THE ROADSIDE

Travelling through the Suian hills, Hsu Yen of Yang-hsien came upon a scholar of seventeen or eighteen. The young man, who was lying by the roadside, said that his feet hurt and asked for a lift in the goose cage which Hsu was carrying. At first Hsu thought he was joking. But the scholar got into the cage, and the cage looked no larger than before while the scholar looked no smaller. He sat down quietly beside the two geese, and they did not seem to mind him. Hsu picked up the cage again, but found it no heavier.

Further on he stopped to rest under a tree and the scholar, coming out of the cage, offered to treat him to a meal. When Hsu accepted with pleasure, the scholar took from his mouth a copper tray laid with all manner of delicacies. The utensils were of copper, and the food had a rare flavour and fragrance. After several cups of wine, the scholar told Hsu:

"I have a girl with me. May I ask her to join us?"

"Certainly."

Then from his mouth the scholar produced a girl of fifteen or sixteen, richly dressed and amazingly lovely, who sat down and feasted with them. Presently the scholar, slightly tipsy, went to lie down.

"Though I have married this man," said the girl to Hsu, "as a matter of fact I hate him. I have brought my lover with me. Now that my husband is asleep, I shall call him out. Please don't say anything."

"Certainly not," agreed Hsu.

Then the girl produced from her mouth another young fellow of twenty-three or four, intelligent and charming, who chatted with Hsu. Just then the scholar started to wake up, and the girl took a silk screen from her mouth to hide the new man. The scholar made the girl join him.

The newcomer told Hsu: "Though that girl is fond of me, I don't care for her. I have brought another girl with me, and would like to see her now. Please don't let them know."

"Of course not."

Then the second man took from his mouth a girl of twenty or thereabouts. They feasted and amused themselves till they heard the scholar stirring.

"Those two are getting up," said the second man.

He popped the girl into his mouth.

The first girl returned and told Hsu: "The scholar is getting up."

She swallowed her friend, and sat alone with Hsu.

Then the scholar came out and told him: "I am sorry I slept so long. You must have been bored sitting here all by yourself. As it is growing late, I will say good-bye."

With that he swallowed the girl and the utensils, leaving only the big copper tray for Hsu. This tray was some two feet across, and in parting the scholar said:

"I have nothing worth giving you, but keep this as a souvenir."

During the Taiyuan period (376-396) Hsu served as an adviser in the Imperial Library and showed the tray to Minister Chang San, who discovered from the inscription that it was made in the third year of Yungping (A.D. 60).

THE FAIRY OF CHINGHSI TEMPLE

When Chao Wen-shao of Kuaichi was the crown prince's steward, he lived near Central Bridge at Chinghsi, about two hundred paces from Minister Wang Shu-ching's house in the next alley. One autumn night superb moonlight made him homesick, and leaning on his gate he sang that melancholy song *Crows Fly in the Night.* Then a maid of about sixteen, dressed in blue, came up to him.

"Greetings from my young mistress in the Wang family," she said. "She heard you sing while we were playing in the moonlight, and sends her regards to you."

As it was still early and not everyone had retired, Chao was not unduly surprised. He answered politely, and invited the young lady over.

In a short time she appeared. She seemed eighteen or nineteen, her gait and air were sweet, and she had two maids with her. Chao asked where she lived.

"Over there." She pointed towards the minister's house. "When I heard you sing, I decided to call. Will you sing something for me?"

Then Chao sang *Grass Grows on the Rock.* He had a clear and melodious voice, and she enjoyed the words too.

"If you have a pitcher," she said, "you need not be afraid of lacking water." She turned to her maids and told them: "Go back and fetch my cithern, and I shall play to this gentleman."

Presently the cithern was brought, and she played two or three haunting and plaintive airs. Then she bade her maids sing *Heavy Frost,* and loosening her belt to fasten the cithern to her waist, played an accompaniment. The song went like this:

Dusk falls, a cold wind blows,
Dead leaves cling to the bough;
Alas, you cannot know
The love my heart holds now!
The curtains of my bed
Are white with heavy frost;
The frost is falling still,
And I alone am lost.

After this song it was late and she spent the night with him, departing at the fourth watch just before dawn. She left him her gold hairpin as a keepsake. In return Chao gave·her a silver bowl and white glass spoon.

When day broke Chao went out and happened to pass the temple. Going in to rest by the shrine, he was surprised to find the bowl there, while behind the screen he discovered the glass spoon. The cithern still had a belt attached to it. In the temple stood the image of the fairy, with maids dressed in blue before her — the same whom he had seen the night before! This took place in the fifth year of Yuanchia (428). But Chao never had another adventure of the kind.

THE YELLOW BIRD

Yang Pao of Hungneng Prefecture was a kind boy. At the age of nine he went to Huayin Mountain and found a yellow bird which had fallen under a tree, badly mauled by an owl. Unable to fly, it was being tormented by ants. Yang Pao took it home with him, and put it on the beam of his room. That night he heard the bird cheeping desperately, and when he took a light to look at it he found mosquitoes were attacking it. So he put the bird in a hat-box and fed it with yellow petals. After a dozen days or so the bird's feathers grew again, and it was able to fly. It would flutter off in the morning and come back at night to roost in the hat-box. This went on for more than a year. One day it brought a flock of other birds, with whom it flew crying round the hall, and several days later it left. At the third watch that night Yang Pao was reading when a boy dressed in yellow came in.

"I am a messenger of the Queen Mother," he announced. "I was on a mission to the fairy isles when I was attacked by an owl. Your kindness saved me. Now I am on my way to the South Seas." Then he gave Yang four jade rings. "May your descendants remain as pure as these rings and reach the rank of chief minister!"

After this Yang Pao's piety became known throughout the empire, and he grew daily more famous and exalted. His son, Yang Chen, begot Yang Ping, who in turn begot Yang Piao. All these four in their generation served as chief minister. When Yang Chen died a huge bird flew down to the funeral, and men attributed this to his great goodness.

THE GOLDEN COCK

Mengkou is near Yutu County in the principality of Nanking, about three *li* west down the river from the county seat. A cave there, shaped like a stone chamber, is called Mengkou Cave. According to the local people, a divine cock, gleaming like the finest gold, appears here. It spreads its wings and flies around crowing until men catch sight of it, when it flies back into the cave. So this is called the Cave of the Golden Cock.

A man was once tilling his fields near the mountain when he saw the cock come out to disport itself. A giant took aim at it with his catapult; but the cock, seeing the giant a great way off, flew inside. The shot simply hit the cave. As the pellet was about six feet across, it blocked up most of the entrance, leaving only a crack too small for men to pass through.

Another man, on his way to this county by boat and still some distance from this mountain, met a stranger in yellow carrying two crates of melons. This stranger begged for a lift, and he took him aboard. When the man in yellow asked for food, the boatman gave him dishes and wine. He had no sooner finished his meal than the boat reached Mengkou Cliff. The boatman asked him for some melons, but instead of giving him melons he spat a mouthful of food on the plate. Then he went up the mountain and disappeared into the cave. Angry as the boatman was, he knew this must be a spirit since it had vanished into the mountain. When he looked at the food spat out by the stranger, he found gold on the plate.

THE MOURNER

In the first year of Yuanchia (424) an artisan named Chu Chin-chih, who had been working on government property in Nankang County, took a boat downstream with his son till they came to a tiny creek. All around was wild and desolate, untrodden by the foot of man. That evening they went ashore and put up in a hostel. There Chu fell ill and all of a sudden died. His son lit a torch and sat up with the corpse. Soon he was amazed to hear wailing in the distance, and a voice lamenting: "Uncle!" In no time the mourner drew near, and proved to be a creature as tall as a man, with hair hanging down to its feet, and on its face neither eyes, nose, mouth nor ears. This creature called the son by name and consoled him, and the boy was so terrified that he heaped all the firewood on the fire.

"I have come to comfort you," declared this monster. "Why are you afraid? Why do you need such a fire?"

It sat by the head of the dead man and mourned. The son stole stealthy glances at it in the firelight, and saw it lay its face against the dead man's cheek. In no time the corpse's face was bare to the bone. The son was appalled and longed to beat it off, but he had no weapon. Then nothing was left of his father's body but bones. Indeed before long both the skin and the bones disappeared. But he never knew what manner of monster this was.

THE MOUNTAIN OGRE

During the first years of the Yuanchia period, a man of Fuyang named Wang set a trap for crabs on a shoal. The next morning when he went to look, all the crabs had gone — in the trap was a piece of wood over two feet long. He mended the trap, throwing the wood on the shore. The next morning the wood was there again and the trap was open once more. Again Wang mended it and removed the wood. But the following morning exactly the same thing happened. Having certain suspicions now of that piece of wood, he put it inside his crab cage, tied this to his pole and started back, swearing to chop the wood up and burn it as soon as he reached home. About three *li* from his cottage, he heard scratching inside the cage and looked round to find the wood had changed into a monkey. It had a human face and only one hand and one foot.

The monkey said to him: "I am so fond of crabs that I have been going to the water and breaking your trap in order to eat the crabs inside. I am extremely sorry. Please forgive me and let me out. I am a mountain god and can help you to catch a great many crabs in future."

Wang retorted: "You have trespassed and committed more than one offence. You deserve to die."

The monkey begged to be released, but Wang turned his head away, ignoring it.

Then the monkey asked: "What is your name?"

It repeated this question again and again, but Wang did not answer. At last, as he was nearing home, it said:

"Since you won't let me go and won't tell me your name, there is nothing more I can do. I shall have to die."

As soon as he was home, Wang made a great fire and burned the monkey in it. No evil consequences followed. The local name for this monkey was "mountain ogre," and it was believed to be able to harm a man once it knew his name. That was why it had asked Wang his name again and again. It wanted to destroy him and so escape.

THE COURT IN THE NETHER REGIONS

In the Hsiaochien period of the kingdom of Sung (454-456), a native of Yingchuan named Yu fell ill and died. His body was still warm and had not been buried when after one night he recovered consciousness, and told the following story.

No sooner was he dead than two men in black appeared, bound him and drove him before them to a great city with high, sheer towers and many lines of defence. Yu was taken into a hall with many others, where a nobleman sat facing south with several hundred attendants who addressed him as their lord. With pen in hand he was checking the names of all arrivals. When he came to Yu, he said:

"This man's time is not up yet."

He dismissed Yu, and an officer came from the steps to lead him out. When they reached the city gate, this officer ordered a guard to send Yu back.

"I must report before you can go," said the guard.

There was a girl of about fifteen outside the gate, a beautiful, elegant creature.

"You are lucky to be going back," she said. "That guard is holding you up because he wants a bribe."

"I left home in such a hurry that I brought no money."

The girl took the bracelet from her left arm and offered it to Yu.

"Give him that."

When Yu asked her name she said: "My name is Chang. My home is at Maochu. Yesterday I was killed by brigands."

119

Yu said: "Before I died I saved five thousand coins to buy a coffin. If I am restored to life, I shall send you that money."

"I am doing this purely out of sympathy. And this bracelet is my own, so you need not return the money to my family."

When Yu gave the guard the bracelet, the latter no longer insisted on going to report, but agreed to escort him back. Yu said goodbye to the girl, who sighed and shed tears. And at that point he awoke. When he made inquiries in Maochu, he found that a daughter of the Chang family had indeed recently died.

THE GHOST WHO THREW COINS

In the third year of the Taming period (459) a man named Wang Yao died of illness in the capital of the kingdom of Sung. After his death the house was haunted by a lean, swarthy ghost bare from the waist up, wearing nothing but a pair of breeches. This ghost used to sing, shout and imitate men's speech, and often threw filth in their food. Then it moved on to some neighbours named Yu on the east, and made the same trouble there.

Yu said to the ghost: "I don't mind you throwing mud and stones at me. If you were to throw money, I really should be put out."

Then the ghost threw several dozen new coins at him, hitting him on the forehead.

"These small, new coins are not so bad," said Yu. "It's the older, larger ones that I'm afraid of."

Then the ghost threw old coins at him. This happened six or seven times, till Yu had more than one hundred coins altogether.

THE LOST SUTRA

Ting Cheng of the principality of Chiyin, whose other name was Te-sheng, served as magistrate of Ningyin during the Chienyuan period (343-344).

One day a woman was drawing water from a well in the north suburb when a man who looked like a foreigner with a long nose and deep-set eyes passed by and asked for a drink. Having drunk the stranger vanished, while the woman was seized with a pain in her belly which grew more and more severe. After groaning for some time she sat up abruptly and issued orders in a foreign tongue. Dozens of the neighbours crowded round to watch. The woman asked for pen and paper, and on being given a pen started writing some foreign script — spidery words that ran from side to side.[1] She covered five sheets of paper which she tossed to the ground, but when she ordered men to read them, not a soul in that district could decipher them. She pointed at a boy of about ten, indicating that he could do it, and sure enough the boy took the papers and read them. The spectators were utterly amazed. Then the woman bade the boy dance, and he stood up, raising his legs and gesturing with his hands. They danced and sang together for a while.

This was reported to Magistrate Ting Cheng, who summoned the woman and the boy. But she told him she had not known what she was doing. Anxious to find out what the writing was, the magistrate sent an officer with it to Hsuchang Monastery where one of the old

---

[1] Unlike Chinese which was written vertically.

monks was a foreigner. This monk from abroad was astounded.

"Part of a Buddhist sutra was lost," he told them. "As we would have had to travel far to seek the original, we were afraid we should never have the complete text. Certain passages we could recite, but not all, and here is the missing part."

It was copied out and kept in the monastery.

IRON MORTAR

During the Sung period there was a native of Tunghai named Hsu, whose wife died after bearing him a son called Iron Mortar. Then he married a daughter of the Chen family, but she was a cruel woman who determined to kill her stepson. She bore a son herself, and at his birth she swore:

"If you don't kill Iron Mortar, you are no son of mine!"

So she named her own boy Iron Pestle, intending the pestle to overcome the mortar. She thrashed her stepson and treated him cruelly, giving him no food when he was hungry and no padded clothes when he was cold. Hsu was a coward, and besides he was often away, so the stepmother had her own way. And at last Iron Mortar died — of hunger, cold and beatings. He was then only sixteen.

About ten days after his death his ghost came back. It went to his stepmother's bed.

"I am Iron Mortar," it said. "Not a soul did I wrong, yet I was cruelly murdered. My mother has lodged a complaint in heaven, and now I am under orders to fetch Iron Pestle. He will suffer as I did and leave this earth very soon. I shall await him here."

The voice was Iron Mortar's to the life. Though the household and their guests could not see him, all could hear him. Then the ghost took up its quarters on the beam.

Hsu's wife kneeled to apologize, slapped her own face and sacrificed to the ghost.

"That is no use," said the ghost. "You starved me to death — do you expect to make up for that with a meal now?"

124

At night she complained in secret.

"How dare you complain of me?" The ghost was angry. "I shall break your roof."

They heard the sound of a saw, and sawdust fell. Then there came a great crash as if the beam had collapsed. The whole household rushed outside. But when they lit a torch to see the damage, nothing at all had happened.

Then the ghost swore at its stepmother: "After killing me, why should you live here in comfort? I shall burn your house down."

They saw a fire belching out smoke and flames, and the whole household was alarmed. But presently the fire died down of itself, and the thatched roof was undamaged. The ghost abused them like this every day, after which it would burst into song:

> Oh, peach blossom and prune blossom,
> What if the frost should cover you?
> Oh, ripe peaches and ripe prunes,
> One frost and all's over with you!

The air was a heart-rending one, as if the ghost were lamenting its early death. Its six-year-old stepbrother had been ill ever since its arrival. His whole body ached, his belly was distended, and he could not eat. The ghost kept beating him too, and wherever it beat him the boy turned black and blue. After a month the child died, and the ghost disappeared for good.

THE MERCHANT'S REVENGE

When Emperor Wu of the Liang dynasty decided to build a monastery at his father's sepulchre, he could not find timber good enough for his purpose. All the local authorities were ordered to make a search.

A rich man of Chu-O named Hung assembled much merchandise with the help of his relatives, and went to Hsiangchow to do business. A year or so later he bought a wooden raft about a thousand yards long, of a rare and magnificent wood. On his return to Nanchin, the local official Meng Shao-ching was so eager to please the court that he heaped accusations on Hung. Because the merchant had some clothing and silk unsold, he was accused of stealing this during his journey. He was also charged with building in a style which violated government regulations. So Meng condemned him to death, and confiscated his raft for the monastery, obtaining government sanction for the execution.

On the day of his execution, Hung bade his wife and children put yellow paper, pen and ink in his coffin, swearing that if he retained consciousness after death he would take revenge. He wrote down Meng's name several dozen times and swallowed the paper with the names on it.

A month later, as Meng was sitting in his office, he saw Hung coming towards him. At first he atempted to evade and resist him. Then he admitted his guilt but begged for mercy. And finally he vomited blood and died. The gaolers and clerks involved in this case died one after the other, until in less than a year all of them had perished.

And the monastery was no sooner built than fire from the sky destroyed it, leaving nothing at all. Even the bases of the wooden pillars, which were set deep under the earth, were reduced to ashes.

HUSBAND INTO SHEEP

A scholar at the capital had a wife who was a jealous scold. She swore at her husband for nothing and pummelled him for a trifle. Moreover she often tied a long rope to his leg, and tugged on this whenever she wanted him. The scholar secretly made a plan with a witch. While his wife was sleeping he went out as if to the privy, fastened the rope to a sheep and jumped over the wall. When his wife woke and pulled the rope, in came the sheep. In horror, she sent for the witch.

"You have done many wicked things, ma'am," said the witch. "Your ancestors are angry. So your husband has been turned into a sheep. If you will repent, I can plead for you."

Then the wife wept bitterly as she caressed the sheep, admitting her fault and swearing to mend her ways. The witch made her fast for seven days during which the entire household had to remain within doors. After that the witch sacrificed to the deities and bade the sheep return to its rightful form, whereupon the scholar came slowly back. When his wife saw him she asked between her sobs:

"Have you had a hard time of it all these days as a sheep?"

"It was unpleasant eating grass, I remember. It made my belly ache."

This made his wife feel even worse. The next time she showed signs of jealousy, her husband dropped on all fours and started bleating. Then she leaped out of bed, bare-footed, and swore by her ancestors that never, never would she be jealous again. So she ceased to be a shrew.

THE LIVE MAN IN THE TOMB

The monk Datta, wanting bricks, opened a tomb and found a live man in it. He presented this man to the court while the empress dowager and Emperor Ming were in the hall of Hualing Park. Feeling that this was unnatural, they asked the imperial steward Hsu Heh:

"Are there precedents for this?"

Hsu answered: "In the Wei dynasty a tomb was opened and found to contain a live slave of Fan Mingyu's family. Fan was the son-in-law of Huo Kuang, who spoke of the rise and fall of the Han dynasty, whose words are borne out by the historical records. There is therefore nothing miraculous about this."

Then the empress dowager told Hsu to ask this man his name, how long he had been dead, and how he had fed himself.

"My name is Tsui Han, my other name Tzu-hung," was the reply. "I am from Anping County in the principality of Poling. My father's name is Tsui Chang, my mother is a daughter of the Wei family, and we lived at Chuntsai Lane in the west city. I was fifteen when I died, and now I am twenty-seven. I have been in the nether regions for twelve years. I felt as if drunk or dreaming, and took no food. Sometimes in my wanderings I believe I saw food, but it was all like a dream — I cannot remember clearly."

The empress sent a clerk called Chang Hsiu-hsi to Chuntsai Lane to look for Tsui's parents, and he found them. Chang asked Tsui Chang:

"Did you lose one of your sons?"

"Yes, my son Tsui Han died at the age of fifteen."

"He has been discovered in a tomb and has come to life. He is now in Hualing Park, and my master has sent me here to make inquiries."

At this the father took fright.

"No, no!" he cried. "I never had such a son. I was lying."

When Chang had reported this, the empress sent him to escort Tsui Han home. As soon as the young man's father knew he was coming, he lit a fire at the gate and armed himself with a sword, while his wife held a twig of peach.

"Don't come here! I am not your father! You are no son of mine! Go away at once if you don't want to get into trouble."

So Tsui Han went away and started roaming the capital, often sleeping at the gate of some monastery. The prince of Junan gave him a yellow garment. Tsui Han was afraid of the light and dared not look up at the sun. He was also afraid of water, fire and arms. He often raced down the road till he was exhausted, but never could he walk slowly; and he was still considered as a ghost.

Most of the inhabitants of Fengchung Lane, north of Loyang Market, sold funeral furnishings and coffins.

Tsui told them: "When you make coffins of cedar, don't line them with mulberry wood." Asked the reason, he explained: "When I was in the nether regions, I saw them conscripting soldiers. One ghost said he had been buried in a cedar-wood coffin, and on that account he ought to be exempted. But the officer in charge said: 'Though your coffin was of cedar, it was lined with mulberry wood.' So he had to join the army after all."

When this story spread through the capital the price of cedar wood soared. Indeed, men suspected that the coffin-makers had bribed him to tell this story.

LADY INTO FOX

North of the market are two lanes called Tzuhsiao and Fengchung, where live the coffin-makers and undertakers. Sun Yen, a professional mourner, married a woman who went to bed fully dressed. She did this for three years, till Sun's curiosity was aroused. One night he undressed her while she was asleep — and found a furry tail three feet long like a fox's brush! Sun was afraid and divorced her; but when leaving she seized a knife, cut off his hair and ran. When the neighbours pursued her she turned into a fox and they could not catch up with her. After this more than a hundred and thirty citizens in the capital lost their hair. The fox would change into a smart, well-dressed woman, and when passers-by were attracted and drew near she would cut off their hair. So any gaily-dressed woman in those days was pointed at as a fox-fairy. This happened in the fourth month of the second year of the Hsiping period (517), but that same autumn these disturbances stopped.

LIU PO-TUO'S WINE

West of the market are two lanes called Yenku and Chihshang, where most of the inhabitants are wine merchants. Liu Po-tuo from Hotung was a most skilful brewer. Even in the hottest part of summer a vat of his wine could be exposed to the sun for ten days without being spoiled. It was delicious and extremely potent: a man could get drunk for a whole month on it. Officials in the capital always took this wine as a present when they went to the provinces, carrying it for hundreds and thousands of *li*, and because it travelled so far it was known as Crane Wine or Donkey Wine. During the Yunghsi period (532-533) Mao Hung-pin, prefect of Nanching, was taking some of this wine to his prefecture when he fell among brigands; but the brigands got drunk on this wine and so were caught. Then it also came to be known as Brigand-catching Wine. And the gallants of that time had a saying:

> Bows and swords you need not fear,
> But of Liu's strong wine keep clear!

THE SPIRIT OF THE RIVER LO

Lo Tzu-yuan of the Imperial Guards, who declared himself a native of Loyang, was stationed at Pengcheng during the Hsiaochang period (525-527). When a fellow guardsman, Fan Yuan-pao, had leave to go back to the capital, Lo asked him to deliver a letter to his family.

"My house is south of Lingtai by the River Lo. Once there you will be met by one of my kinsmen."

Fan did as he was asked. But he found no houses south of Lingtai. He was about to leave when an old man approached and asked:

"Where are you from? Why are you wandering here?"

Fan told him the reason.

"That is my son," said the old man.

He took the letter and led Fan towards lofty halls, spacious pavilions and magnificent houses. After Fan had taken a seat, his host ordered a maid to bring in wine; and soon, to Fan's astonishment, she walked past with a dead child in her arms. The wine served was red in colour and had a fine bouquet. There was excellent food as well, the greatest delicacies of sea and land. After feasting, Fan said farewell and the old man saw him out, expressing regret that they might never meet again and seeing him off in a most friendly manner. As soon as the old man went in, the buildings disappeared. Nothing was left but the high river banks and the water flowing eastward. Then Fan saw a newly drowned boy with blood flowing from his nostrils, and realized that it was this lad's blood that he had just drunk. When he returned to Pengcheng, Lo had disappeared too. Though they had served as guards for three years together, Fan had never known that his friend was the spirit of the River Lo.

PRINCE TAN'S REVENGE

Prince Tan of Yen was a hostage in the state of Chin. When the king of Chin slighted him he wanted to leave, but the king would not hear of it.

"Not until crows turn white and horses grow horns!"

The prince looked up and sighed. Thereupon crows turned white and horses grew horns, and the king of Chin was forced to let him go. He set a trap on the bridge for the prince; but when the prince crossed the bridge the trap broke down. The prince reached the pass at night while the gate was still closed; but by crowing like a cock he got all the other cocks to crow, and so he made good his escape. He nursed a deep grudge against the king of Chin, and burned to avenge himself. To this end he spared no effort to gather brave men around him.

The prince wrote to his tutor, Chu Wu: "Your humble student was born in a poor, barren, petty state. Nor have I mastered the learning of those who are wise and high-minded. I have a wish, however, which I beg you to consider. I have heard that a man should think it shame to live on after being insulted, and a woman should think it shame to be violated and lose her chastity. This is why they are willing to have their throats cut or be thrown into boiling cauldrons. It is not that men love death and set no store by life, but that they have integrity. Now the king of Chin has flouted the will of Heaven like some savage wolf or tiger. He has treated me worse than all the other princes: the thought of this tortures me to my very marrow. As I see it, my forces are not enough to oppose him and I have not the strength to wage a protracted war. I therefore mean to gather all the brave men under heaven and all the gallants within the four seas, spending my state's entire resources to keep them. Then with honeyed words and rich gifts I shall approach the king of Chin. If he covets my gifts and trusts my words, one single swordsman will prove a match for a million armed men, and one brief moment will wipe out my everlasting shame. How otherwise can I face the world during my life, or be free from regret after death in the nether regions? The princes will point the finger of scorn at me, and my territory north of the River Yi will fall into alien hands. This will bring disgrace on you too. Hence I am sending you this letter, and hope you will give it due consideration."

Chu Wu sent him this reply: "I have heard that a man who follows the dictates of his heart acts unwisely and against nature. Your Highness is eager to vent your anger and avenge a grudge. But though I should not mind grinding my bones to dust to achieve this, to my mind a wise man does not rely on luck, an intelligent one is not carried away by his feelings. We should take action only when sure of success and bestir ourselves only when it is safe, to avoid imprudent behaviour and calamities. I think Your Highness imprudent to stake everything on the courage of a single swordsman. I would suggest instead that we ally ourselves with the kingdoms of Chu, Chao, Han and Wei before opposing Chin. Then our enemy can be defeated. The states of Han and Wei seem on friendly terms with Chin, but this is only skin-deep. If we start a war and Chu follows, I have no doubt that Han and Wei will join in. This is clearly the situation. If you follow my advice, you can wipe out your shame and lighten my burden too. I hope you will consider this."

The prince was not pleased with this reply, and summoned his tutor to discuss the matter.

Chu Wu said: "I believe if Your Highness acts on my suggestion, our territory north of the River Yi can never be threatened by Chin and all the neighbouring states will look up to us."

"But all this will take time, and I cannot wait."

"I have given this matter serious thought. So long as the state of Chin exists, it is better to act slowly than hastily, better to sit and wait than race ahead. Though time will be needed to form alliances with Chu, Chao, Han and Wei, these tactics are bound to succeed. I do, indeed, consider this your best course."

The prince did not listen, pretending to be asleep.

Then Chu Wu said: "I cannot help Your Highness. But I know a man called Tien Kuang, who is very wise and an excellent strategist. May I send him to Your Highness?"

To this the prince agreed.

When Tien Kuang came for an audience, the prince welcomed him on the steps and bowed before him. And after they had taken seats he said:

"Though our state is uncultured and I am ignorant, my tutor has asked you to our humble domain. Our kingdom lies far to the north, near the barbarians, yet you have consented to come and I can gaze on the wonder of your countenance. I attribute this condescension on your part to the protection of the gods above."

Tien Kuang replied: "Ever since I came of age and knotted my hair, I have admired your high-minded conduct and your great fame. What instructions has Your Highness for me?"

The prince advanced on his knees, shedding tears as he did so.

"When I was a hostage in the state of Chin, the king of Chin treated me discourteously. So day and night my heart burns for revenge. But Chin has more men and much greater strength than Yen, and my heart recoils from the thought of alliances. I have lost my appetite and cannot sleep. Even if my kingdom perishes with Chin, I shall feel as if dead ashes were burning again and white bones restored to life. I hope you will advise me."

"This concerns the safety of a state. Allow me to think it over."

The prince lodged Tien Kuang in the best hostel, served him daily with food and supplied his every need. When this had gone on for three months, the prince was surprised that Tien Kuang still made no proposal. He went to him, dismissed his attendants and said:

"Since you took pity on me and promised to give me your advice, I have been waiting for three months for your proposal. Are you willing to advise me now?"

"I would have done so to the best of my ability even if Your Highness had not asked me. I have heard that when a fine steed is young a thousand *li* is nothing to it, but when it is old and jaded it cannot stir. Your Highness has condescended to consult me, but I am too old to act. I could give you advice, not that Your Highness wants it, but feats requiring strength are beyond me. None of your men appear suited for the task in hand. Hsia Fu has courage in his blood: when he is angry his face turns red. Sung Yi has courage in his veins: when he is angry his face turns green. Wu Yang has courage in his bones: when he is angry his face turns white. But I know a man named Ching Ko who has superhuman courage. When he is angry he does not change colour at all. He has wide knowledge, a retentive memory and great strength. He cares nothing for trifles, but longs to achieve great deeds. He used to live in the land of Wei, where he has helped more than a dozen noblemen. No other man is worth considering. If you want action, Ching Ko is the man for you."

The prince rose from his seat to bow.

"If through your kindness I can meet this man, my state will endure for ever. Will you help me?"

Then the prince saw Tien Kuang off, taking his hand to say:

137

"The future of my kingdom is at stake. I beg you not to disclose this to anyone."

"Rest assured." Tien Kuang gave a smile.

Then Tien Kuang went to Ching Ko and said to him: "I have taken the liberty of recommending you to Prince Tan. The prince of Yen is a genuinely great patron, who has the sincerest admiration for you. I hope you will not doubt this."

Said Ching Ko: "My motto is: If I like the man I will risk my life for him. If not, I will not part with a single hair. Since you want me to befriend the prince, I shall obey you implicitly."

"A gentleman should not lay himself open to suspicion. When the prince saw me off, he told me that the future of his kingdom was at stake and begged me not to disclose his secret. This means that he does not trust me. I should be ashamed to live on as an object of suspicion."

In front of Ching Ko he swallowed his own tongue and died. Then Ching Ko set off for the land of Yen.

When Ching Ko reached the state of Yen, the prince served as his charioteer, leaving the left-hand seat for him. And Ching Ko took the reins without declining. They seated themselves at the feast among many guests.

Ching Ko said: "Tien Kuang has praised Your Highness's magnanimity and nobility. Your fine conduct and great reputation fill men's ears and have reached to the sky. This is why I left the land of Wei and came to the land of Yen, not counting the journey long or difficult. Now Your Highness is treating me as an old friend and welcoming me with every mark of respect; but I do not decline the honour, for I know Your Highness understands my worth."

"Is Tien Kuang well?" asked the prince.

"When he saw me off he told me that Your Highness had warned him about some secret of state. Ashamed that you could not trust him, he swallowed his tongue and died before my eyes."

The prince was shocked and changed colour. He sobbed, but presently restrained his tears.

"I warned him not because I suspected him. Now that he has killed himself, I shall stand condemned by the whole world."

Deeply grieved, he remained lost in thought for some time. Then he urged Ching Ko to drink, and when they had eaten their fill the prince rose to propose a toast. But Hsia Fu stepped forward and said:

"I have heard that if a gentleman is not praised in his own district, one need not consider his moral character. If a horse cannot draw a carriage, one need not consider its speed. Now Ching Ko has come from a great way off — what good advice has he to give Your Highness?"

This was a challenge to Ching Ko, who replied:

"A gentleman of outstanding ability may not suit the local taste. A horse which can gallop a thousand *li* may never have drawn a carriage. When Lu Wang worked as a butcher and fisherman, he was low in the eyes of the world; but after meeting King Wen he became the leader of the army of Chou. When a fine steed is harnessed to a salt cart, it is a sorry sight; but when it meets a charioteer like Po Lo it can gallop a thousand *li*. A good man need not be recognized by the men of his district, nor a fine horse tested on a carriage."

Hsia Fu asked again what advice he had for the prince.

Ching Ko answered: "I shall help the state of Yen to carry forward the tradition of Duke Shao of Chou and his benevolent influence, and to match the three ancient kings or at very least the five famous conquerors. What do you say to that?"

All present applauded this speech, and throughout the feast no one could put him down. The prince was delighted, convinced that with Ching Ko he need no longer fear the king of Chin.

Later they went to the pond in the east palace. When Ching Ko picked up a stone to throw at the frogs, the prince ordered his men to bring a plate of gold. Ching Ko threw the gold into the water piece by piece.

"I will stop now," he said at last, "not to save your gold but because my arm is tired."

Then they rode out on mettlesome chargers that could gallop a thousand *li*.

Ching Ko said: "I hear that the liver of steeds like this is delicious."

The prince at once had a horse killed and presented him with the liver.

At that time General Fan Yu-chi of Chin had offended the king and come to Prince Tan for refuge. The prince gave a feast in his honour at Huayang Tower, during which a beautiful girl played skilfully on the lyre.

"What fine hands she has!" remarked Ching Ko.

The prince offered the girl to him, but he replied: "It is only her hands that attract me."

Then the prince had her hands cut off, and presented them to Ching Ko on a jade plate. The prince ate at the same table with him and slept on the same couch.

When some time had passed and Ching Ko was at leisure, he said:

"I have served Your Highness for three years, and you have treated me most handsomely, giving me gold to throw at the frogs, feeding me with the liver of your finest horse and presenting me with the beautiful hands of your maid on a jade plate. Even a low brute, shown such honour, would do his best to serve Your Highness in some humble capacity. I, who have enjoyed the company of gentlemen and learned from gallant men, know that life and death may be as meaningless and light as a feather, or as significant and weighty as a mountain. All depends on how a man employs his time. I beg Your Highness to instruct me."

Then the prince adjusted his garments and spoke gravely.

"When I was in the land of Chin the king insulted me. I cannot bear to live while he draws breath. Now that you have honoured my small state with your presence, inferior though I am I mean to entrust my kingdom's future to you. I am at a loss for words to express myself."

Ching Ko said: "No kingdom in the world today is more powerful than Chin. You are not strong enough to awe the other states and they will not serve your need; while if you oppose Chin with your own men only, it will be like hunting a wolf with a sheep or pursuing a tiger with a wolf."

"This has long preyed on my mind, but what can I do?"

"General Fan Yu-chi has offended the king of Chin, and they are most eager to lay their hands on him. Chin also wants our territory in Tukang. If I can have General Fan's head and the map of Tukang, all will be well."

"To accomplish this I would gladly give my whole state. But General Fan came to us for refuge in time of danger. I cannot betray him."

Ching Ko was silent.

Five months later the prince, fearing Ching Ko was unwilling to go, said to him:

"Now the king of Chin has conquered the state of Chao and is threatening us with his arms. What can we do to save the situation? Shall we send Wu Yang first?"

"Only a coward would refuse to go if asked by Your Highness!" Ching Ko was very angry. "I delayed because I was waiting for a friend."

Then he went secretly to General Fan.

"I hear you have offended the king of Chin. Your parents, wife and children were burned to death, and the king has offered a fief of ten thousand families and

141

a thousand pounds of gold for your head. I pity you. But I have a proposal for wiping out your disgrace and avenging the state of Yen. Do you care to hear it?"

Said General Fan: "This is constantly on my mind. Day and night I choke back my sorrow, not knowing how to take revenge. What is your plan?"

"I would like to have your head and the map of Tukang. If I present these to the king, he will be pleased and grant me an interview. Then with my left hand I shall seize his sleeve and with my right I shall pierce his heart, after denouncing him for wronging you and the state of Yen. Then Prince Tan's disgrace will be wiped out and you will be avenged."

General Fan rose, grasped his wrist and drew his sword.

"This is what I have been waiting for day and night! Now I know what I should do."

He severed his own throat, and his head dangled down his back, his eyes open and staring. When the prince knew of this, he drove there in his chariot. He fell on the corpse and wept. Overcoming his grief at last, he put the general's head in a casket to be sent with the map of Tukang to the king of Chin. Wu Yang was to accompany Ching Ko.

Instead of choosing an auspicious day, Ching Ko set off at once. The prince and the others who were in the plot dressed in white to see them off on the bank of the Yi. Then Ching Ko offered a toast and sang:

> The wind is wailing
> Cold the river shore;
> The heroes who depart
> Come back no more!

Kao Chien-li played the cithara and Sung Yi sang the accompaniment. The heroic strains made men's hair stand on end with anger, while the sad ones drew forth their tears. Then the two men mounted their chariot

142

without once looking back. When they passed, Hsia Fu died at his own hands to bid them farewell. In the city of Yangtse, where they stopped to buy some meat, because Ching Ko disputed the weight the butcher insulted him and Wu Yang tried to pick a quarrel; but Ching Ko stopped him. They journeyed west to the land of Chin till they reached Hsienyang. Then they sent this message to the king through a nobleman named Meng:

"The prince of Yen, awed by Your Majesty's might, presents the head of General Fan and a map of Tukang to show that he wishes to be your vassal in the north."

The king of Chin was pleased. Attended by all his officers and hundreds of halberdiers, he granted the envoys of Yen an audience in court. Ching Ko carried the general's head, Wu Yang the map. While drums and bells sounded, all the officers cheered. Wu Yang was too terrified to walk a step, and his face turned deadly pale — to the king's astonishment. After one look at Wu Yang, Ching Ko stepped forward.

"He is a barbarian from the north," he apologized, "and has never seen such pomp and majesty. I beg Your Majesty to overlook it, so that we can carry out our task."

"Bring the map here yourself!" ordered the king.

When the king unrolled the map, the dagger appeared. Then Ching Ko with his left hand seized the king's sleeve, and with his right pointed the dagger at his heart.

"You have long wronged the prince of Yen!" he cried. "You are an insatiable tyrant. General Fan committed no crime, yet you wiped out his clan. I am here to avenge them all. The prince of Yen has a proposal for you. If you agree to it, you can live. Otherwise you must die."

"I shall agree to any proposal you make. But let me hear some music before I die."

He ordered one of his maids to play the lyre. What she sang was this:

> A robe of silken gauze
> May be quickly torn;
> A screen not six feet high
> May be overborne;
> A sword upon the back
> May be seized and drawn!

Ching Ko did not understand the drift of this song, but the king acted upon it. Drawing the sword on his back, he tore his sleeve, jumped over the screen and ran. Ching Ko hurled the dagger at him, piercing one of his ears. When the dagger struck the bronze pillar it sent out sparks. Then the king came back and cut off both Ching Ko's arms. Ching Ko leaned against the pillar and laughed. Squatting down, he swore at the king.

"Because I took this too lightly, the fellow has fooled me. I am only sorry not to have avenged the prince and to have failed in my task!"

TALES OF EMPEROR WU

Travelling incognito, the emperor once went to Poku. He wanted to spend the night at the local station-house, but when the station-master would not admit him he put up at an inn.

The innkeeper said: "A sturdy fellow like you should work hard in the fields. Why travel at night with a sword and a band of men? You must be planning robbery or rape."

The emperor remained silent and did not answer. Presently he asked for some wine, and the innkeeper said:

"We have no wine here — only piss."

With that he went inside. The emperor sent men to watch him, who found him gathering together a dozen or so young men with bows and arrows and swords; and he told his wife to go out and keep the travellers from leaving. By and by the old woman went back and said to her husband:

"This man looks something out of the ordinary. Besides, he is well prepared. You had better treat him politely instead of attacking him."

"This is easy," replied her husband. "If I sound the drum and gather more men against these brigands, I have no doubt but that we shall defeat them."

"Be careful then. Wait till they've gone to bed."

The old man agreed.

The emperor had about a dozen followers with him. Hearing this plot they were afraid and begged him to slip away in the night. But the emperor said:

"If we leave there will be trouble. We had better stay to calm them."

145

Then the woman came out and asked the emperor: "Did you hear what my husband said? Crazy old drunkard! Don't you worry, though. Tonight I promise you a quiet sleep."

She went inside again, and as it was very cold she plied her husband and the young fellows with wine until they were drunk. Then she tied the old man up and the others ran away. Finally she came out to apologize to the guests, and killed a chicken for them. At dawn the emperor left. On his return to the palace that day he summoned the innkeeper and his wife, gave the woman a thousand pounds of gold and made her husband an imperial guardsman. But this was a lesson to him, and he never travelled incognito again.

Emperor Wu once went to the guardsmen's office. There he saw a white-bearded and white-haired old man in shabby clothes.

"How long have you served here?" asked the emperor. "How is it you are so old?"

"My name is Yen Ssu," was the reply. "I am from Chiangtu. I joined the guards in the reign of Emperor Wen."

"Why have you never been promoted in all these years?"

"Emperor Wen cared more for the arts of peace, while I was trained in those of war. Emperor Ching preferred older men, and I was too young for him. Now Your Majesty prefers younger men, and I have become too old. So for three reigns I have never been promoted, but am still an old guardsman in this office."

The emperor was touched, and appointed him military tribune of Kuaichi.

In the second year of the Shihyuan period,[1] constables reported that utensils for imperial use had been stolen by common citizens. When the inscriptions were ex-

---

[1] 85 B.C., two years after Emperor Wu's death.

amined, it appeared that these things came from Emperor Wu's tomb — they had been bought in the market. Marshal Huo Kuang suspected the officers in charge of the burial of negligence which permitted thieves to rob the tomb. He accordingly had the chief officer arrested and tried in the capital.

More than a year later in the county of Yeh another jade cup came into the market. The officer in charge suspected that this was imperial property, but before he could make an arrest the man selling it disappeared. When the cup was taken to court, they found it was also from Emperor Wu's sepulchre. Marshal Huo Kuang questioned the officer himself, and his description of the man in the market sounded strangely like Emperor Wu. The marshal said nothing, but quietly pardoned the workmen who had been imprisoned.

A year later the emperor revealed himself again and said to Hsueh Ping, the officer in charge of the sepulchre:

"Although my reign is over, I am still your sovereign. How dare you allow your men to sharpen their swords on my tomb? See that this does not occur again."

Hsueh Ping kowtowed and apologized, whereupon the apparition disappeared. When Hsueh made inquiries, he found a square stone by the sepulchre which could be used as a whetstone, and there his men often sharpened their swords in secret. When the marshal knew of this he wanted to have Hsueh killed. But he forbore when Marquis Chang An-shih reasoned with him:

"The ways of spirits are not as the ways of men. We need not take them as laws."

In Kanchuan Palace bells and drums were sometimes heard when no musicians could be seen, and the attendants often saw retinues with the full imperial equipage. But by degrees these ceased to appear, stopping once for all in the reign of Emperor Hsuan.

ANECDOTES CONCERNING TSAO TSAO

When Tsao Tsao was young he often went out with Yuan Shao in search of adventure. Once they saw a wedding in progress, and crept into the bridegroom's courtyard. At night they shouted: "Thief! Thief!" When everyone rushed out from the bridal chamber to catch the thief, Tsao Tsao went in with his sword to kidnap the bride, and then made off with Yuan Shao. They lost their way and Yuan Shao fell among brambles and could not get out. Then Tsao Tsao cried:

"Here's the thief!"

Yuan Shao leaped with fright, and so they managed to escape.

When Yuan Shao was a youth, he sent a man at night to throw a dagger at Tsao Tsao. The dagger was aimed too low and hit the couch. Guessing that the next throw would be aimed high, Tsao Tsao lay as flat as he could, and the second attempt failed too.

Tsao Tsao once said: "No one must come near me when I am asleep. If anyone does, I will cut him down with my sword in my sleep. Let all my followers beware!"

Later he pretended to be asleep, and when one of his favourite ladies tiptoed up to cover him with a quilt, he cut her down and killed her. After that whenever he slept no one dared go near.

In one of his campaigns Tsao Tsao failed to find a watering place, and all his troops were suffering from thirst. Then he announced that there was a great plum orchard ahead, the trees laden with sweet and sour fruit which could quench thirst. Hearing this his men's mouths watered, and they managed to struggle on to their destination.

Tsao Tsao claimed that he always knew when anyone wanted to harm him. And he told one of his favourite followers:

"Come to me with a dagger on you. I will say I have a premonition of danger, and have you arrested to be killed. But just say nothing about this trick, and no harm will come to you. In fact I shall reward you well."

That fellow trusted him and had no misgivings. Then Tsao Tsao had him killed, and that man did not realize till his death that he had been deceived. All Tsao Tsao's followers thought his sense of danger was genuine, and conspirators were disheartened.

One day Tsao Tsao had to receive a Hunnish envoy. Afraid that he did not look distinguished enough to overawe this barbarian, he ordered Tsui Yen to take his place while he stood by the couch holding the sword. After the audience he sent a spy to ask the envoy:

"What did you think of our prince?"

"Your prince is a striking figure," replied the envoy. "But the man with the sword by the couch is a true hero."

When Tsao Tsao heard this, he sent pursuers to capture and kill the Hun.

THE MAN WHO RISKED HIS LIFE
FOR HIS FRIEND

Hsun Chu-po travelled a great distance to see a friend who was ill. The place was being attacked by the Huns when he went.

"I shall die here," said his friend. "You had better go."

"I came all this way to see you," retorted Hsun. "And now you tell me to leave! How can I act against my conscience simply to save my skin?"

The invaders came and said to him: "At our great army's approach the whole district has fled. Who are you that dare to stay here?"

Hsun replied: "My friend is ill and I cannot leave him. Let me beg you to take my life instead of his."

Then the Huns said: "We are wicked men coming to the land of the just."

They withdrew their troops and the whole district was spared.

THE CORAL TREE

Shih Chung and Wang Kai rivalled each other in extravagant display: their clothes and equipage were as magnificent as possible. Since the emperor was Wang Kai's nephew, he often assisted him. Once he gave him a coral tree over two feet high with many branches, the like of which Wang had never seen before.

Wang Kai showed this to Shih Chung, who took one look at it and then smashed it with an iron wand. Wang Kai grew heated over the loss of this treasure and disgusted at Shih's envious behaviour.

"Don't worry," said Shih Chung.

He told his attendants to fetch his coral trees. Six or seven of them were more than three feet high, with superb branches and a dazzling colour, while he had many more as good as that of Wang Kai.

Wang Kai felt considerably chastened.

TUNG-FANG SHUO THE JESTER

Once the nurse of Emperor Wu of the Han dynasty committed some offence outside the palace, and the emperor was about to punish her. She asked Tung-fang Shuo to help her.

"This cannot be argued," said the jester. "But if you really hope to succeed, look at the emperor again and again as you are being led away. Don't say anything though. This is your only chance in a thousand."

When the nurse was brought in, Tung-fang Shuo was also present.

"You are a fool," he said to her. "How could the emperor remember your former kindness? He was a child when you were nursing him."

The emperor, despite his ambition and ruthlessness, was a man of feeling. Moved with pity, he pardoned the nurse.

THE THREE EVILS

When Chou Chu was a young man, his savage temper and love of adventure made all his countrymen fear him. Havoc was caused in the district of Yihsing by a serpent in the lake and a tiger in the mountain. So the local people spoke of their Three Evils, counting Chou the worst of the three. Someone advised him to kill the tiger and the serpent, hoping in this way to get rid of two of the evils. First Chou Chu killed the tiger, then he plunged into the lake to grapple with the serpent. The monster came to the surface and submerged again, swimming many *li*, but Chou stayed close beside it. After three days and three nights the local people thought he must be dead, and were indeed congratulating themselves when Chou came back after finally killing the serpent. When he heard men speaking joyfully of his death, he realized that he, too, was considered a pest and determined to mend his ways.

He went to the district of Wu to look for the Lu brothers. Failing to find Lu Chi, he sought out Lu Yun and explained to him that he wanted to mend his ways, but after so many wasted years it seemed too late to change.

Lu Yun said: "The superior men of old thought it good to know the truth even if one had to die that very evening. And you are still in your prime. Moreover a man should worry if he has no ideal in life, not if he has no fame."

Then Chou Chu corrected his faults, and became a loyal and a pious man.

WANG HUI-CHIH'S IDIOSYNCRASIES

Wang Hui-chih once lodged for a short time in an empty house belonging to another man. He ordered bamboos to be planted there.

Someone asked: "Why take so much trouble when you are staying here for such a short time?"

Wang merely recited poetry for a while, then pointing at the bamboos asked:

"Can one live a single day with this gentleman?"

One night when Wang Hui-chih was living in Shanyin there was a heavy fall of snow. Upon waking and opening his door he ordered wine to be served. He gazed around at the expanse of white, and strolled up and down reciting Tso Ssu's poems on a hermit's life. Then he suddenly remembered Tai Kuei, then in Yen County, and set out that same night in a small boat to visit him. The journey took one whole day; yet when he reached the door he turned back instead of entering.

Asked the reason, he said: "I set out on a happy impulse. Now that mood is over, I am going back. What need was there to see him?"

LIU LING THE DRUNKARD

One day Liu Ling had too much to drink, but feeling parched he asked his wife for more wine. She poured away the wine and broke the pitcher, and with tears in her eyes advised him against tippling.

"You are drinking too much — it is bad for your health. You must stop it!"

Liu Ling said: "Very well. But I cannot control myself. The only way is to swear before the gods to give it up. Prepare the sacrificial meat and wine."

His wife agreed to this.

She placed wine and meat before the shrine and asked Liu Ling to make his oath. Liu Ling knelt down and prayed:

"Heaven gave me life and made me famed for drinking. I drink ten pints at a sitting, and five will cure my headache afterwards. A man should not listen to the words of a woman."

Then he drained the wine and ate the meat, and soon was drunk again.

WEN CHIAO'S SECOND MARRIAGE

Lord Wen Chiao was a widower. A distant aunt of his named Liu, whose family had suffered in the wars, had an only daughter — a pretty, intelligent girl. Her mother asked Wen Chiao to find her a husband, but he was eager to marry the girl himself.

"It is hard to find a good match," he demurred. "What would you say to some man like myself?"

His aunt replied: "After the trouble we have seen, all I want is enough to live on — that is all I hope for in my declining years. How can I aim so high?"

A few days later he told her: "I have found a man. His family is respectable and he is a noted official, no less well known than I."

He sent a jade mirror-stand as betrothal gift, and his aunt was overjoyed.

After the wedding ceremony, the girl pushed the fans aside, clapped her hands and laughed.

"I guessed it would be this old fellow. I suspected as much!"

The jade mirror-stand was a trophy presented to Wen Chiao when he served under Liu Kun in the northern expedition against Liu Tsung.

THE LOVER WHO SCALED A HIGH WALL

Han Shou, Chia Chung's secretary, was a handsome man. One day when Chia Chung held a council, his daughter saw Han through the window and fell in love with him. She began to pine for him and to write love poems. Her maid went to Han Shou's house and told him this, dwelling on the remarkable beauty of her mistress till Han's interest was aroused. He begged the maid to take a secret message, making a tryst to visit the girl at night. And being very agile, he climbed over the wall into her house without her family's knowledge.

After this, Chia Chung observed that his daughter took a great interest in her appearance and seemed to be strangely elated. Later, during an assembly of all his officers, he detected a rare perfume about Han Shou's person. This perfume was part of the tribute from abroad: a single application retained its fragrance for months. And since the emperor had given this scent to Chia Chung and Chen Chien alone, no one else could have it. Accordingly Chia Chung began to suspect that Han Shou was having an affair with his daughter. But the house was surrounded by high walls, and the passages and doors were narrow. How could anyone get in? On the pretext that he had been robbed, he ordered workmen to repair the walls. They reported that every part was in good condition except the north-east corner, where there appeared to be footprints, though the wall was too high to climb. Then Chia Chung questioned his daughter's maids, and learned the truth from them. He kept it a secret, but married his daughter to Han.

TWO COMMENTATORS

Fu Chien had made a careful study of the *Chou Dynasty Annals* and was writing a commentary on this work, but wanted to compare notes with some other scholar. When he heard that Tsui Lieh was giving his students lectures on the subject he hired himself to Tsui as a cook, not disclosing his real name. He listened to the lectures outside the door. And when he found that Tsui's knowledge was no greater than his own, he started discussing certain points with the students. Tsui had no idea who he was, but knowing Fu Chien's reputation he suspected that this was he. One day he went to him at dawn and called his name while he was still asleep. Taken by surprise, Fu answered. Then they became good friends.

A TALENTED BRIGAND

Tai Yuan was a wild young fellow who loved adventure. He turned brigand in the Huai River Valley and held up passing merchants. One day he ordered his young men to rob Lu Chi, who was travelling back to Loyang on leave with considerable luggage. Tai sat on the bank on his couch to issue orders, directing the operation with great skill. And since he was outstandingly intelligent, even as a brigand he behaved with distinction.

"You are a man of great ability," called Lu Chi from his boat. "Why should you be a brigand?"

Then Tai Yuan was moved and threw away his sword to join Lu Chi on his boat. His original mind commanded the other's respect. They became sworn brothers and Lu Chi recommended him to the court. After the imperial house of Tsin moved south of the Yangtse River, Tai Yuan was appointed a general.

A WIFE'S ADVICE

When Hsu Yun of the Wei dynasty was in the Ministry of Civil Affairs, he employed so many men from his own district that Emperor Ming sent guards to have him arrested. His wife gave him a warning.

"You may convince His Majesty by argument, but on no account plead for mercy!"

When he entered the imperial presence, the emperor questioned him.

Hsu Yun replied: "A man should recommend only those whom he knows well. I know my fellow countrymen. Your Majesty can investigate to see if they discharge their duties competently or not. If they are not up to their work, I shall plead guilty."

Then the government investigated these men and found them competent. So Hsu Yun was released. And since his clothes were torn and soiled, the emperor presented him with new.

When Hsu Yun was arrested the whole of his household had wailed except his wife.

"There is no cause for alarm," she said calmly. "He will be back."

She made some broth against his return, and sure enough before long he came home.

THE SOLDIER WHO LOVED WINE

During the revolt of Su Chun, the entire Yu family fled. Yu Ping, then governor of the district of Wu, was deserted by all his officers and men. He escaped alone with one of the district soldiers, who rowed him down the River Chientang hidden under some matting in a little boat. As Su Chun had offered a reward for Yu Ping and his men, a strict search was in progress. The soldier moored by an island to go ashore for a drink. Coming back, drunk, he waved his oar at the boat.

"Who is looking for Governor Yu? I have him here!"

Yu Ping was horror-struck and dared not move. But when the officers in charge saw that the boat was too small to carry much and the soldier was completely drunk, they suspected nothing. They let the craft proceed to the River Cheh, where Yu Ping found refuge with the Wei family of Shanyin. In this way he escaped death.

The revolt once over, he decided to reward the soldier. He asked him what he wanted.

"I come from a humble family, so I want no rank or insignia," was the answer. "I have worked hard at low tasks since my boyhood, and often been sorry that I could not drink my fill. All I ask is wine to last me to the end of my days."

Then Yu Ping had a large house built for him, bought him slaves, and saw to it that he had always a hundred pints of wine. So all men said that this soldier was not merely intelligent but knew how to live.

APPENDIX

The Source Books for This Selection

PRINCE TAN'S REVENGE (YEN TAN TZU 燕丹子)

This book is first mentioned in the *Sui Dynasty History.* Its date and author are unknown. Some scholars believe it was written after the second century; others place it earlier.

TALES OF EMPEROR WU (HAN WU KU SHIH 汉武故事)

Attributed to Pan Ku 班固 (32-92) of the Han dynasty, and also to Wang Chien 王俭 who lived towards the end of the fifth century. The book is incomplete.

TALES OF MARVELS (LIEH YI CHUAN 列异傳)

Attributed to Emperor Wen of Wei 曹丕 (186-226), also to Chang Hua 張华 (232-300). It was probably written in the third or fourth century.

RECORDS OF SPIRITS (SHOU SHEN CHI 搜神記)

Attributed to Kan Pao 干宝 who lived at the end of the third and the beginning of the fourth century.

ACCOUNTS OF IMMORTALS (SHEN HSIEN CHUAN 神仙傳)

By Keh Hung 葛洪 (290-370).

RECORDS OF STRANGE THINGS (PO WU CHIH 博物志)

Attributed to Chang Hua 張华 (232-300).

RECORDS OF GHOSTS AND SPIRITS (LING KUEI CHIH 灵鬼志)

By a certain Hsun 荀氏 probably of the fourth century.

MORE RECORDS OF SPIRITS (SHOU SHEN HOU CHI 搜神后記)

Attributed to Tao Chien 陶潜 (365-427).

TALES OF CHI HSIEH (CHI HSIEH CHI 齐諧記*)*
   By an unknown author of the fourth or fifth century.

RECORDS OF LIGHT AND DARK (YU MING LU 幽明录*)*
   By Liu Yi-ching 刘义庆 (403-444).

NEW ANECDOTES OF SOCIAL TALK (SHIH SHUO HSIN YU
      世說新語*)*
   By Liu Yi-ching 刘义庆 (403-444).

TALES OF JEALOUS WOMEN (TU CHI 妬記*)*
   By Yu Tung-chih 虞通之 of the fifth century.

RECORDS OF WONDERS (LU YI CHUAN 录异傳*)*
   By an unknown author of the fifth century.

MORE TALES OF CHI HSIEH (HSU CHI HSIEH CHI 續齐諧記*)*
   By Wu Chun 吳均 (469-520).

ACCOUNTS OF MARVELS (SHU YI CHI 述异記*)*
   Attributed to Jen Fang 任昉 (460-508).

DIVINE MANIFESTATIONS (MING HSIANG CHI 冥祥記*)*
   By Wang Yen 王琰 of the sixth century.

ACCOUNTS OF AVENGING SPIRITS (YUAN HUN CHIH 寃魂志*)*
   By Yen Chih-tui 顏之推 (531-?).

A RECORD OF THE TEMPLES OF LOYANG (LO YANG CHIA
      LAN CHI 洛阳伽藍記*)*
   By Yang Hsuan-chih 楊衒之 of the sixth century.